PENGUIN BOOKS

WHAT IT FEELS LIKE FOR A GIRL

'A truly fresh, exciting take on the

'Paris Lees's novelised account of h
make you shake with laughter and w
of a few pages' *British Vo*

'Powerful and authentic, a memoir with the depth and writerly
virtuosity of a fine novel' Katherine O'Donnell

'Paris Lees has created a totally complete world in the way that
something like *Trainspotting* or *Skins* or *It's A Sin* did . . . made a universe,
populated it with people that you absolutely care about, dialect that
you're completely absorbed by, then smashed your heart to smithereens'
Alexandra Hemingsley

'A ketamine-laced coming of age memoir . . . green backlit Nokia
phones, Bacardi Breezers, Gap jeans, retired slang, Nike Air Max
trainers . . . a dark comedy from a little-heard perspective . . .
very powerful' Kadish Morris, *Observer*

'Shocking, funny, heart-rending and brilliant' *Daily Mirror*

'Fast and funny and furious . . . the writing is so alive and warm
that you don't feel remotely miserable while reading it, even while
your heart is pounding for her' Sophie Heawood, *Grazia*

'A sensational, gut-wrenching read: raw, moving, and
ultimately life-affirming' Owen Jones

'Often hilarious, sometimes moving, consistently engrossing, always
authentic and ultimately uplifting. Reminiscent of *Trainspotting* and
Irvine Welsh. A tour-de-force' Matt Cain

'A bold and compulsively readable autobiography' *Harper's Bazaar*

'Heartbreaking, hilarious and impossible to put down:
Paris Lees' *What It Feels Like For a Girl* is genuinely singular.
It's raw, viscerally real and Byron is a character who will stay with
you long after you've finished' Yomi Adegoke

'Paris Lees is the voice of a generation' Paul Flynn

'Raw, heartbreaking, and scorchingly funny, *What It Feels Like For A Girl* is a boldly-written and truly transformative account of an extraordinary life story. Please do yourself a favour and read it' Otegha Uwagba

'An important debut' Édouard Louis

'Lees has lived an extraordinary life, and it makes for extraordinary writing' Rebecca Nicholson, *Guardian*

'A must-read . . . as mesmerising as it is poignant' *Stylist*

'Heartbreaking and hilarious' *Dazed Magazine*

'It is so vivid, and the use of dialect so clever, that it feels as if you are living her life with her' David Walliams

'Like Alan Sillitoe on acid . . . it's got to be a film. I've never read anything like it' Vicky McClure

'Raw and original' *Elle Magazine*

'Clever, gripping, messy, sad. I loved it' Travis Alabanza

ABOUT THE AUTHOR

Paris Lees was born in Hucknall, Nottinghamshire. She is a Contributing Editor at British *Vogue*, and has written for the *Guardian*, *VICE* and the *Telegraph*. She has received multiple awards for her journalism and work as an anti-bullying campaigner – and an honorary doctorate from the University of Brighton. She was the first openly trans woman to present on BBC Radio 1 and Channel 4 and also the first to appear on *Question Time*. This is her first book.

What it Feels Like for a Girl

PARIS LEES

PENGUIN BOOKS

PENGUIN BOOKS

UK | USA | Canada | Ireland | Australia
India | New Zealand | South Africa

Penguin Books is part of the Penguin Random House group of companies
whose addresses can be found at global.penguinrandomhouse.com.

First published by Particular Books 2021
Published in Penguin Books 2022

001

Copyright © Paris Lees, 2021

The moral right of the author has been asserted

Printed and bound in Great Britain by Clays Ltd, Elcograf S.p.A.

The authorized representative in the EEA is Penguin Random House Ireland,
Morrison Chambers, 32 Nassau Street, Dublin D02 YH68

A CIP catalogue record for this book is available from the British Library

ISBN: 978–0–141–99308–9

www.greenpenguin.co.uk

Penguin Random House is committed to a
sustainable future for our business, our readers
and our planet. This book is made from Forest
Stewardship Council® certified paper.

For Mister Duck

Be thou the rainbow to the storms of life!
— Lord Byron

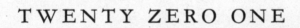

TWENTY ZERO ONE

YOU DON'T KNOW ME

The vicar sez Lord Byron worra bit of a gay boy an' I had to bite ma tongue so I din't burst out laughin'. Sez he worra right bogger. After we left, Old Mother 'ubbard guz, "He din't mean what you're thinkin', duck. He meant he worra rogue. A ladies' man. Someone wi' loose morals." I thought, OK, but they do say he were bisexual. An' he were into that black magic. Serves 'em right for namin' me after 'im, eh? I were born on the exact same day as 'im, two hundred years later. We're Capricorns.

It's a nice name, innit? I wonder where they could possibly have got the idea from. Oh yeah, I forgot. Everythin's called Byron round here. Byron Taxis. Byron Cinema. Byron Bingo. At the end of our road there's even a pub called – wait for it – The Byron. Smanfa's brother guz, even though he's only just turned sixteen. They don't check or nowt. It gets dead busy at weekends. Blokes always come an' piss outside our house comin' back from the boozer on Friday nights. I watch 'em through the net curtain an' try an' gerra good look. It's bad, innit?

Lord Byron's buried in the Parish Church of St Mary Magdalene in 'ucknall – an unbelievably, indescribably, mind-bendingly borin' town in the Nottinghamshire countryside that folk say got shut down wi' the mines in

3

the eighties. The people are small-minded an' the streets are paved wi' dog shit. He were menna go in Westminster Abbey with all the other important people, but they said he were too risqué. So they brought 'im back here, to slowly rot away wi' the rest of us. I think about 'im sometimes, in 'is crypt, an' 'is tattered old clothes. He were dead pale-lookin'. I reckon he'd make a great vampire.

He'd be in good company. Most people round 'ucknall look like they've lost the will to live. They just shuffle about like the livin' dead, goin' on about kitchens they're too skint to do up or marriages they're too scared to leave. Not that there's owt else to do. There's a Wilkos an' a flea market, an' that's yer lot. Nothin' ever happens — an' no one ever leaves. But d'ya know what I hate most about people round here is? They lack aspiration. Mammar Rita sez I'm "precocious" when I talk like that. Mammar Rita's ma dad's mam. Mammar Joe's me mam's mam — but I call 'er Old Mother 'ubbard coz she's always "runnin' low on supplies", apart from Giro day. Gaz sez, "There's no need to gi' yersen airs an' friggin' graces just coz yer a clever clogs," but I don't even reckon I am that clever. I just think everyone else round here's stupid.

Ben Caunt's buried in St Mary's too. He worra famous boxer in Victorian times. They named Big Ben after 'im. Gaz sez he's a local hero. OK so how come he died in London? An' how come Lord Byron died in Greece? They say 'is heart's buried out there. He said England could have 'is body, but yer heart's what makes ya who ya are. So it is possible to escape. He were rich, though. An' Ben Caunt were the strongest man of 'is time. Last

4

time I checked, I'm neither. Mary Magdalene were mates wi' Jesus, but Mammar Joe sez she were just as bad as Byron. She worra prostitute! So how come they named a friggin' church after 'er?

I live at 26 Annesley Road, 'ucknall, an' ya can see St Mary's from here – an' quite a bit of it if ya happen to be havin' a sneaky fag out the back window in the attic, like I am. It's five to five an' when the bells start I'm gonna see if I can run downstairs before the last one. You've literally got five seconds. I nearly did it the other day. Mammar Rita sez I'm gonna end up breakin' ma neck if I'm not careful an' she might be on to summat, but I can't miss the start of *Ready Steady Cook*, canna? It's ma favourite programme. Well, after *Big Brother*. Ya can watch 'em in the shower if you've got the internet! Which we don't, obviously, coz Gaz don't seem to realize there's bin a cyber revolution an' a new Millennium an' that.

No wait – it's *Absolutely Fabulous*. That's ma favourite TV show ever.

I've gorra change this shirt, though. I've got coal stains on it again. I lost ma key last month so I've had to climb in through the coal grate for the past fortnight. If I go to the shop or take the dog out I leave the back door on the latch an' hope he don't notice, which so far he an't. I'm not tellin' 'im. He'd go mental.

That's 'im now, pullin' up outside the DIY store next-door-but-one. He drives a black Golf GTI. Ya can hear it comin' down the road from a mile off, screechin' or purrin' dependin' on what mood he's in – if he slams the door, yer in real trouble. Ya don't mess wi' Gaz Lees, not if ya wanna keep hold of yer teeth, ya don't. He's the 'ardest man in 'ucknall. And, unfortunately, *ma father.*

Gaz is thirty-three an' spends 'is weeknights weight-liftin', badger baitin' an' findin' things that have fallen off the backs of lorries. On weekends he starts fights outside the Wine Bar, 'ucknall's most sophisticated drinkin' establishment. Gaz is the 'ead bouncer. He's under the impression that people round here respect 'im, but they're just scared of 'im. He thinks it's the same thing. 'Is favourite film's *Braveheart.* That's how he sees 'issen.

Gaz has three kids wi' three women, an' possibly more we don't know about, accordin' to me mam. They all "respect" 'im too. He's always gerrin people preg-nant, sometimes two at once. Mam sez it's the only bit he seems to like about parenthood. Ma lil' brother's mixed race. He's an equal opportunities womanizer, our Gaz, an 'orrible bastard no matter who ya are.

Gaz never guz to parents evenin', which is funny coz he's always goin' on about how "Education is the key ter the world" – like he'd know owt about that! I don't even think he can read an' write. I know he don't write ma birth-day cards coz ya don't have to be Sherlock Holmes to recognize Mammar Rita's handwritin', an' the nice mes-sages are a bit of a giveaway, too. No, I reckon the closest Gaz Lees has come to gerrin a certificate is havin' 'is name put in the cane book. Mr Smith remembers 'im. Mam's in there too, claim to fame or what? God knows why they think I'm gonna behave any better than they did!

I'd better open this window a bit wider. I don't tell Gaz nuffin, although he must know I smoke coz I'm always goin' in 'is leather jacket an' nickin' 'is Benson an' Hedges. They come in a gold packet so they're quite posh for 'im. I think they're the ones ya put in them cigarette holders they used to have in Olden Times, ya know, like what Joan Collins'd smoke. I've always wanted one. An' them long gloves they had, dead glamorous an' that. I get Superking Blacks usually coz they're big an' ya can have half an' save the rest for later. I tried a Menthol at break once – like Dot Cotton off of *EastEnders* – an' ended up runnin' outta German five minutes later an' throwin' up in the yard.

Gaz knows ma mates smoke. He come back once after we'd bin smokin' weed an' were like, "What ya on with in here, then?" I blamed Smanfa. Smanfa's ma best mate. 'Er name's actually "Samantha Bennet", but no one calls 'er that, like how no one sez the H in 'ucknall. He were like, "Yo' must think Ah fell off a friggin' Christmas tree", so he must be on to me coz he's not completely completely stupid an' I'm sure I've heard 'im tell Mammar Rita he's tried weed before, an' yer'd *never* forget the smell o' that, would ya? So if he knows I smoke da reefer, he must know I smoke fags. He don't know where I get the money for 'em, though.

YOU SEE THE TROUBLE
WITH ME

D'ya remember that advert for oven chips? That little girl goin', "Daddy or chips, daddy or chips", tryna make 'er mind up coz 'er sister asks 'er which one she prefers. Well, she chooses chips, don't she? Obviously. Coz it's a fuckin' chip advert. Even though 'er dad looks dead nice an' giz 'er a kiss on the cheek. I don't know anyone whose dad's like that in real life. Gaz just knocks me about an' calls me a fuckin' poof. Smanfa's is an alcoholic.

We never have oven chips. Sometimes Gaz giz me a fiver an' sends me to the chippy up the road, but only coz he's too lazy to go 'issen. An' coz he's gorra feed me. They'd take me away if he din't, but no such luck. Ma favourite's the "special". Chips, kebab meat, chicken, salad, mayo an' chili sauce, all in this big polystyrene box. They don't do that at every chip shop, ya know, so I'm lucky to live nearby when ya think about it. Sometimes I'll have fish, chips an' mushy peas. Or fish cake. Or chicken an' mushroom pie. Oh, an' a can of Coke, if I can afford it. Gaz hardly ever cooks, which suits me coz I hate 'is cookin'. Truth told, I hate everythin' about 'im. Burra love chips!

The thing is though, chips cost money an' money don't grow on trees, accordin' to Gaz. Did I say it did? Not that I'd ever dare be that cheeky out loud, mind.

People say money can't buy ya happiness but I'm not so sure. No one round here's got any anyway, so how the hell would they know? An' would ya rather cry yer eyes out in a massive mansion or a council house? I know what I'd prefer. Some of 'em are dead scruffy. Like next door, for example. Dirty bastards.

Mam's place is nice. It's the best house on the estate. Not like there's loadsa competition or nuffin – Amy next door sez they only have a bath once a week an' 'er little sister wipes 'er bum on 'er skirt! – but Mam keeps our place dead clean. I have to have a bath every night. I don't mind, though. I quite like it, actually. An' when I say clean, I mean clean. She's obsessed, ma mother. She's got good taste, though. We've got nice furniture an' that, although I don't live with 'er any more, unfortunately.

She cut the end of 'er finger off when I worra baby – on this big machine at some factory she worked for – an' got loadsa compensation money. Two thousand pounds, an' that were in the eighties. 'Er index finger. That's the one ya use all the time. Sliced the tip right off. She said the skin grew back, like how a spider's leg does if ya pull it off. I don't know why anyone would wanna do that, but it's amazin' what yer body can do, innit? The doctor sez she were lucky it missed the bone. So now she's got nice carpets an' one finger's shorter than the rest. An' underlay. Not everyone has underlay round here. Underlay, underlay! Speedy Gonzales!

Well, I'm not at ma mother's now – that's another thing Gaz loves tellin' me. Oh Gaz, don't I know it. He found out about ma radiator the other day. I were laid in bed when I noticed water comin' out of it. Turned out there worra little hole in it, so I phoned Smanfa an' she were like, "Try an' block it up wi' some chewin' gum", but it wun't stick. Ma floor were gerrin wet, so I had no choice. I had to tell 'im.

He went mental, obviously. Sez I've done it. I said how could I have done it? He guz, "Ya've bin messin' abaht up there." I'm like, "Dad, how could I make a hole in metal?" So he giz me a clip round the earhole an' tells me not to be cheeky. But it worra genuine question. He sez I've bin throwin' darts at it or summat. How could I have bin throwin' darts? I an't even got any darts. Who the fuck has darts these days? That's the sorta thing Uncle Andy'd have, from Olden Times, like dominos. I don't need darts. I've gorra Walkman for fuck's sake!

Smanfa sez he's bein' ridiculous. She wants to tell 'im I honestly din't do it, but I won't let 'er coz it'll only make 'im worse. Well anyway, the upshot is he's turned ma radiator off now coz he sez he "can't afford to fork out for a new 'un". So it's dead cold in ma room, an' it's all ma fault, of course. An' I'd better keep ma mouth shut if I know what's good for me, blah blah blah.

SMACK MY BITCH UP

Jamie Draper's halfway down the field wi' that twat who looks like a pig. Don't know 'is name. Let's call 'im Pork Chop. Two years above an' I'm pretty sure he's bin expelled before. They both have. Proper little scruff-bags. It looks like they're goin' towards the jitty but I don't think they've seen me. I'm gonna slow down an' wait for 'em to piss off.

But as I turn into the alleyway they're just stood at the other end, waitin'. There's a woman with a pram comin' past, but once she's gone they're gonna start on me, I know they are. Fuck's sake. Worram I gonna do? I can't show 'em I'm scared. I'll just have to carry on walkin', won't I? But I am fuckin' scared. But it's like, why should I have to go the long way home all the time? If I turn back now though, it'll be dead obvious I'm frightened an' they'll tell everyone. Then they'll all know what a massive pussy I am. As if they don't already.

I should've just turned back before she left, I could've forgotten summat. How would they know? I should've just swallowed ma pride, coz really, who cares if they think I'm a big poof? Everyone keeps tellin' me I am, so I must be. I deserve it. I deserve to be beaten up. They block me. "Sorry, poofters aren't allowed past. There's lil' kids on this estate." I try an' play it cool, try to be matey.

11

Big mistake. "Yeah, I am a big poof – so ya don't wanna be seen talkin' to me, do ya?" So then he's like, "Are ya bein' cheeky? Coz Ah'll smash yer face in, ya fuckin' bender." I'm scared, but if I try an' razz it now they'll just run after me an' trip me up, so I just stand there, shakin', not knowin' what to do. Why did I come this way?

They're laughin'. Pork Chop's got big blotchy cheeks the colour of ham. He's thick as shit an' looks like one o' them that sniffs glue, but who's the stupid one here, really? Me, for comin' this way, that's who. Thank God I an't got ma Walkman wi' me coz Jamie's goin' for ma baseball cap like, "Byron the Bender, what ya got this for?" an' knocks it off ma 'ead. "D'ya really think they'd let faggots like yo' play baseball? Mind you, yer'd love that, wun't ya? Goin' in the showers with all the blokes an' pervin' on 'em." I go to pick it up, but he kicks ma arm, an' then Pork Chop snatches it. Jamie's like, "Urgh, don't touch it, you'll get AIDS!" So Pork Chop's like, "Fuck off!" an' chucks it. An' I'm thinkin', Why are ya doin' this? Why can't ya just let me be? "Here ya are," he guz, "there's some dog shit there. Gerrit in that."

I beg 'im not to but Jamie boots me in the shin with 'is Caterpillars an' wrestles me to the ground. He's got me in a headlock an' I don't bother fightin' back coz what's the fuckin' point, eh? It'll only make 'im worse. He's shoutin' to Pork Chop, "Go on, gerrit in the shit!" Ma face is pressed into the grit. There's bits of broken glass every-where and, at the bottom o' the hedge, an empty packet of crisps that's bin faded by the sun. I can just make out an old bloke on the other side o' the field with 'is dog, but he's too far away to see us. An' I'm just so angry wi' mysen coz I've got tears in ma eyes an' I've let 'em get to me. An' now they're laughin' at me, enjoyin' every minute of it.

Pork Chop kicks ma hat in the shit. Ma New York Yankees cap that Mam bought me for Christmas. That I'll never be able to wear again now. Jamie's like, "Ya wanna fuckin' fight?" So I'm like, "No, I just wanna go home, please let me go, Jamie." That just makes 'im worse. "Don't say ma name, Ah'm not yer boyfriend, ya fuckin' bender." Pork Chop's cryin' wi' laughter by now an' askin' me why I talk like a girl. Then he punches me in ma 'ead, ma face, ma eye. Ma fuckin' eye! Then he smacks me in ma nose – hard! Reckon he's gone an' broken it. Fuck's sake! Pork Chop's kickin' me too an' I try an' break free, but I just end up gerrin ma legs caught in the brambles instead.

But then someone's shoutin', "Oi, leave 'im alone!" an' I can see the woman wi' the pram comin' back. "Go on, pack it in 'fore I call the police!" They look at each other an' just burst out laughin', then Jamie gobs in ma face. Proper snot. I wanna throw up. Pork Chop grabs ma hat an' puts it on ma 'ead. I just can't believe this is happenin', but more fool me, eh, coz I should be used to it by now. An' I'm thinkin', You bastards. I'm gonna be rich an' famous one day, an' I hope ya read about me in the paper an' how fuckin' fabulous ma life is. "What's up?" he guz. "Ah thought ya liked shit!" Then Jamie's like: "D'ya cry when yer bummin' an' get shit on ya bell-end? Oh sorry, Ah forgot, ya prefer bein' bummed, don't ya? D'ya cry when yer gerrin fucked up the arse?" Pork Chop guz, "Nah, bet he loves it!" An' then they run off.

I'm shakin'. The woman pulls up with 'er pram an' asks me if I'm alright. I've gorra nosebleed. An' dog shit in ma fuckin' hair! An' I've ripped ma jeans, or rather they've ripped ma jeans. Ma Gap jeans! So I can't even keep this secret now. I'll have to explain how I've gorra hole in 'em. I wanna disappear, I want the ground to just open up an' swallow me. I've heard people say that on telly, "I just wanted the earth to swallow me whole." Well, I know exactly what they fuckin' mean now. I hate ma life, I hate livin' here an' I hate bein' me.

All ma stuff's come out ma bag so she bends down an' helps me pick it up. She sez, "What they pickin' on ya for?" So I tell 'er they're callin' me gay an' she's like, "Oh, whadda they know, eh?" but then she sees ma Vengaboys pencil case an' guz, "And anyway, so what if y'are." She's dead nice. I wish I were grown up like 'er so I din't have to deal with all this shit. Actual fuckin' shit. Dog shit! In ma fuckin' hair. I can't walk all the way to Gaz's like this, though, so I'm gonna have to go to me mam's, but I can't find ma fuckin' key. Fuck's sake.

I don't wanna sit on the front where everyone can see me, so I go round the back, but Pop's next door feedin' 'is pigeons. I don't wanna talk to 'im either, so I just stay by the side door an' hope Amy don't come out coz then

I really would look fuckin' stupid. An' she'd tell every-one. That'd be fuckin' perfect, eh? So anyway, then Mam comes back an' starts gerrin dead upset. She's on about callin' the police so I'm like, "Please don't, Mam, it'll only make it worse."

"Alright, I'm callin' Gaz."

"No! Please don't, Mam!"

"Gaz or the police. Ya can't let 'em get away with it, Byron – I'm not 'avin' it!"

I've got blood on ma jumper an' ma nose is throbbin'. I'm sick o' this, sick of all of it. Is it not enough that I have to sit on ma own? Eat on ma own? Walk home on ma own? That *everyone* hates me? That I get laughed at an' spat on an' punched every fuckin' day? Am I gonna be tormented like this for the rest of ma life? Coz I can't stop bein' who I am, canna? An' anyway, what have I done wrong? Who am I hurtin', eh? Why can't people just fuck off an' leave me alone?

They split up when I worra baby. I don't remember 'er bein' with 'im. He used to come round for a bath sometimes an' sit there in a towel till I went up to bed, but that were years ago. Weirdo. The only other time I used to see 'im were when he come to pick me up from Mammar Joe's an' take me to Mammar Rita's for Sunday dinner. Aunty Ray sez I used to scream an' grab 'er legs when I saw 'is car at the end o' the road. She'd beg Mammar Joe to let me stay but she'd just say, "It's not ma decision, Ray. He's gorra go!"

I went to live with 'im when I were nine coz Mam cun' control me any more. They've both got tempers on 'em. Mammar Joe sez I gerrit from them. It's a pity they din't have loadsa money for me to inherit too, innit? Mammar Joe sez it's a wonder I turned out alright "wi' Lisa for a mother an' Gaz for a father", but I reckon she might be callin' it a bit too soon. Mr Smith sez he can see me goin' either way – sez I'm either gonna do summat dead good wi' ma life, or dead bad. He's just not sure which. So that's nice, innit? Mr Smith has long grey hair an' loves Queen. He's the only person I've heard say owt nice about Margaret Thatcher.

I were dead naughty when I were little. I bit Old Mother 'ubbard in Safeways once. I feel bad about it now.

She threatened to hit me with 'er belt when we got home, but she din't. I don't think she'd ever be 'orrible like that, she's lovely to me. Mammar Joe's more like me mam than me mam. She were dead young when she had me mam, an' me mam were dead young when she had me.

Mam slept on a mattress in the livin' room for six months when I were little an' din't wanna talk to anyone or do owt, so I had to wait for Mammar Joe to bring me ma tea after school. Mam sez Primula cheese is common but Mammar Joe would say, "Ma sandwiches, ma rules", coz she knows they're ma favourite. Gaz said, "Yer mam's got some bleddy nerve", an' "Beggars can't be choosers if she can't be arsed ter feed ya 'ersen", but I don't remember 'im ever bringin' owt round. I'd sit an' look out ma bedroom window till I saw Mammar Joe comin' across the field. Always wearin' summat black an' soup-stained, like the witch in *Simon an' the Witch*. I'd go, "Don't ya get tired walkin' all that way?" She'd go, "Ner, ne' mind. Kill the owd 'uns off first, eh?" Owd's how Mammar Joe pronounces "old". She's forty-seven.

I love Old Mother 'ubbard. I stay with 'er every weekend. She gets 'er Giro on Thursdays so I go after school on Fridays an' she does me a tray with a Pot Noodle an' a Freddo an' a tangerine. Well, Mam definitely don't like Pot Noodle, but Mammar Joe sez what she don't know won't hurt 'er. She lets me stay up an' watch *Father Ted* too. We love Mrs Doyle. She's dead funny. Mammar Joe even lets me watch Graham Norton sometimes, but never *Eurotrash*. She sez I shun't be watchin' stuff like that. She sez they shun't even be airin' it.

Mammar Joe looked after me when me mam went to live in Turkey. She come back after three months coz it had all gone wrong. Tarkan turned out to be 'orrible like Gaz in the end, an' took all 'er money off 'er. She had to save up secretly to buy a ticket back. Mammar Joe sez it's a pity me mam's superior taste don't seem to apply to men, but me mam sez men all are the same no matter where ya go anyway. Gaz calls it doin' a Shirley Valentine. He's always goin' on about it, how she's such a bad mother an' that. Like he's father o' the friggin' century! He's gorra point, though. I thought she'd left me for ever.

I don't wanna tell 'em what's happened, but how can I lie? I've bin beaten up. They want details. "Why din't ya smack 'em one back?" he guz. "Ah've told ya ter stand up for yersen." I can't look 'im in the eye, so I just stare at the telly. Summat bad's gone off in America so instead of kids TV, the news is on. They're showin' these two skyscrapers wi' smoke comin' out of 'em. I think a plane's crashed into 'em or summat, but the sound's down so I can't hear what they're sayin'. "Oi, Ah'm talkin' to ya!" Hang on, why is *he* mad wi' *me*? I'm the one who's bin beaten up here. But that's typical Gaz, innit? – of course it's all ma fuckin' fault.

Mam's goin', "He's not like you, Gary!" An' then he starts shoutin', "Yeah, an' why's that? All ma other kids are normal – it's your juices that've made 'im like this. Nowt wrong wi' ma sperm." 'Er juices! Fuckin' hell. I'm like, "Aunty Ray sez ya can't solve violence wi' violence." So he's like, "Aunty Ray talks out 'er friggin' arsehole!" which is a bit rich, comin' from 'im. Talk about the pot callin' the kettle black. "Yeah, but if someone punches me once, they might leave me alone then. But if I hit 'em back, they're just gonna keep on smackin' me."

"Not if ya knock 'em out, they won't. Not just stand there like a great big fuckin' poof." Here we go.

"But what if I don't wanna get dragged down to their level?"

I shun't answer 'im back, but I can't believe he's mad at me. It's just so unfair!

"Ah've told ya before an' Ah'm tellin' ya now, next time someone hits ya, ya hit 'em back – twice as 'ard. An' stop actin' like a fuckin' gel."

The Van pulls up outside. Pete's Mobile Van. Five o'clock he comes, just as *Ready Steady Cook*'s startin' an' everyone's home from school. Mam usually lets me get a Kinder Egg if I've bin good. Amy next door always gets a Freddo. She makes out it's 'er favourite, but really it's coz they're dead poor an' Freddos are only fifteen p. Sometimes she just gets a ten-p mix. "I can't, I'm not strong like you!" He jumps up an' throws me on the settee, fists up. "What ya gonna do if someone hits ya?"

"Nuffin!" I go.

So he whacks me!

"What ya gonna do if someone hits ya?"

"Nuffin!"

Whack!

Looks like I'll be missin' the *Fresh Prince* today.

SCREAM IF YOU WANNA
GO FASTER

He clouts me round the ear again an' I can't help but flinch, which just makes 'im even worse. He don't like weakness. He grabs ma hair an' me mam's screamin', "Gaz, leave 'im alone, he's just bin beaten up, for God's sake!" But is he fuck gonna leave me alone now. "Stay out o' it, yo'," he guz, an' I wonder if she's next. She knows there's no point arguin', but she's goin' on about callin' the police an' how she wishes she'd never rung 'im an' wants 'im out o' 'er house. But ya did ring 'im, din't ya? Hate to say I told ya so, Lisa, but I did fuckin' beg ya not to.

"What ya gonna do if someone hits ya?"

He's hurtin' ma hair so much I'm scared he's gonna pull it out.

'Nuffin. I'd rather be punched by someone than punch someone else.'

Whack!

"What ya gonna do if someone hits ya?"

An' then, all of a sudden – an' I can't explain it – I just start laughin'. An' I'm calm. Alert, but calm. It's like summat's shifted inside me, an' I don't care any more. Like I'm floatin', an' lookin' down at the room. An' it all just seems just so ridiculous. Ma 'ead's pulled back an' ma arms are up out of instinct an' I'm thinkin', D'ya know what, maybe yer on to summat. Maybe I should start standin' up for mysen. Coz what's there to be scared of, really? What could possibly be worse than this? Ma father's a bastard, ma mother's an idiot, an' everyone hates me. What's to lose? So I look 'im straight in the eye, an' I tell 'im, "Smash ma 'ead in if ya like. Kill me! But I'd rather die than be like *you!*"

He lets go of me instantly an' drops back into the armchair. I don't know what's just gone off. Mam's speechless. I've never known 'er to be this quiet in ma entire life. I realize how much noise we must've bin makin' an' wonder if Pop next door can hear us, coz I reckon she's wonderin' it too. All she fuckin' cares about is what the neighbours think, so that's backfired today. I look around the room an' everythin' looks different. It's like the air's changed. Gaz is cryin'. "Why can't ya be normal?" he guz. "There's summat wrong wi' ya. Yer a problem child."

Oh I'm a problem child, am I? I've heard it all before – from 'im, from people at school – but it's like I'm really hearin' it this time. Like I'm finally gerrin the message everyone's bin tryna tell me ma whole life. There's summat wrong wi' me. I an't gorra problem. I *am* the problem. Me. The way I talk. The way I walk. Everythin' about me's wrong. I am wrong. Just for existin'. But this is great news! Coz if there's summat wrong wi' me, why should I even try to be good? Coz if I'm not normal, I can be – an' do – whatever I want. An' what I want – what I really, really want – is to get out o' this fuckin' hell-hole. An' everyone else can go fuck 'emselves.

Mammar Rita brought me a blanket the other day. I told 'er the radiator weren't ma fault. I think she believes me but she started goin' on about how all teenagers fall out wi' their parents an' "At the end o' the day, he is yer dad!" as if I'm not already fully aware o' that. Then she's on to 'er all-time favourite: "He does love ya, ya know? He's just gorra funny way of showin' it." Well no, I *don't* know that, actually, Mammar Rita, but if he does it's a very funny way indeed, almost like the complete opposite. If this is 'is love, God know's what 'is hate must feel like.

They had it much worse when Mammar Rita were young, though. There were no central heatin' so I should count mysen lucky, really, apparently. She had to put 'er fur coat on the bed in winter! Oh, but also, at the same time, everythin' were so much better back then. People din't lock their doors coz there were no crime, accordin' to 'er, an' if ya saw a stranger walkin' down the street, well, ya just invited 'em in for a brew! I have a feelin' folk wun't have bin flingin' their doors open an' pourin' tea down yer neck if ya happened to be gay, or black or even just a single mam, but if Mammar Rita sez it were better back then, it must have bin. She were there an' I weren't. People kept their net curtains white in them days. Din't matter if yer kids were bein' abused in the back room an' yer 'usband knocked ya about a bit, so long as yer front porch were scrubbed clean everythin' were perfect.

Mammar Rita's right about one thing, though. He *is* ma dad. But that don't make any o' this better. If anythin', it makes it *worse*. Coz if ya love someone, ya shun't be 'orrible to 'em. Gaz is always goin' on about how, "Yer've gorra be cruel ter be kind", but aren't ya also supposed be *kind* to be kind? Ya know, even just every now an' then? Mammar Rita sez I should respect 'im an' it just makes me so mad. So what, coz he got Mam pregnant thirteen years ago, that means I've gorra look up to 'im for the rest of ma life? No matter what he does to me? No matter what he sez to me? Sorry Mammar Rita, but I really don't think so.

I'm movin' out as soon as I'm sixteen an' then no one'll be able to tell me what to do. I'll go to London an' have loadsa men after me like Samantha from *Sex an' the City*. An' if Gaz comes anywhere near me, I'll kill 'im. Literally. I'll get a baseball bat an' batter the old bastard. An' I'm takin' the dog wi' me too. Poor old Benji, he's in a really bad state. Covered in cuts. Gaz took 'im fox huntin', or maybe it were badger baitin' coz I've never seen 'im this bad. It's horrendous. I don't know how anyone could take pleasure from makin' animals fight to death. I went to see 'im earlier an' he were just stood there, shakin'. Gaz won't let 'im inside, not even while he gets better, coz he shat in the back room last Christmas. So he's in the doghouse – guess that makes two of us. I ought to call the RSPCA but I can't, canna? He'd know. I mean who else'd call 'em? Next door wun't dare.

I wish Benji would just run off. I let 'im off the lead when I take 'im up the hill but he always comes back, daft bogger. Just as well I s'pose coz then I'd be in even more trouble, although I wun't mind if I knew he'd found some nice people to look after 'im an' give 'im cuddles an' that. I wish he could talk. I'd tell 'im he don't have to stay here, that he could just like . . . run away.

DON'T CALL ME BABY

You'll never guess worrav had for ma birthday. I din't wanna go home after school, so I went to the toilets on 'ucknall Market an' locked mysen in a cubicle. I just wanted to be somewhere quiet. D'ya know worra I mean? I do that at school sometimes, find an empty room or the loos no one uses, an' just go an' sit there. I like bein' somewhere ya can hide. I'd bin in there for about half an hour readin' the graffiti – there's loadsa pictures of nobs an' all this stuff about a girl called Stacey Parker who's a right old slag by the sounds of it – but when I come out, the same bloke that had bin there when I went in were still stood at the urinal. He looked like he were up to no good, so I went an' sat on the wall outside an' waited for 'im to come out. But he never did. I were sat there ten minutes coz I watched the church clock get to five an' I thought, Am I goin' crazy? So I went back in an' he were just stood in the same place. I din't know what to do, so I ran into the cubicle an' locked the door.

I sat there thinkin', What the fuck am I gonna do now? I felt embarrassed coz he'd seen me come an' go, an' I thought, I bet he thinks I've got diarrhoea. But then I thought, Why should I feel stupid? An' what the bleddy hell is he up to? Then he tries the friggin' door! When there were two other cubicles free! I thought, Oh my God, I've gorra right weirdo here, an' right as I'm thinkin' it he puts 'is hand under the door. Ma heart were thumpin'. I thought, What if he's a murderer? But then I thought, Fuck it, so I undid the latch an' he pushed it open. I were thinkin', Oh God, please don't let me die in 'ucknall Market bogs.

He must have bin about forty. He wore denim 'ead to toe an' had a bottle of whisky in 'is back pocket – he stank o' fags an' booze. Blond, an' scruffy-lookin', bit of a hippy type. But quite good-lookin'. He reminded me of a cowboy. He din't look gay. Not like how ya see on the telly an' that. An' he din't say owt either, he just gor-rit out an' . . . well. He wanted me to pull ma trousers down too, but I were too embarrassed. He put 'is hands down there, though.

I've bin goin' every day after school. They call it "cot-tagin'". Don't ask me why. They do it all over the place, apparently. Gaz'd go mental if he knew. Good. I can't believe all this has bin happenin' five minutes away from where I live all this time an' I din't even know. Right next to the church! It's a wonder no one catches 'em. Most of 'em are married an' all. It's bad, innit? Imagine if their wives knew what they were up to! I bet some of 'em have got kids too. An' I'm just there, in ma uniform, an' they don't even care. Ma uniform!

But here's the best bit – they gi' ya money! I daren't stand at the urinal, I'm too scared, so I just go an' sit in the cubicle an' wait for someone to try the door. The next time I went, there were an old bloke in there, so I din't undo the latch. He put 'is hand under the door, but

I just ignored 'im. So five minutes later he put a note under sayin' "How much". It took me a while to work it out, but then he waved a fiver under the door. I were excited, but I thought, I'm gonna need a bit more than that for you, mate. But I realized, I've got summat they want. An' it's up to me if I give it 'em or not. An' that giz me power.

Smanfa's auntie's a prostitute. She stands on the corner of Forest Road an' waits for cars to pull up. Apparently she guz, "Are ya lookin', darlin'?" As in, "Are ya lookin' for me to suck yer cock in exchange for an as-yet-to-be-agreed sum of cash?" Ya can't just say that, though, can ya? It's like a game. In case it's the police or summat. Everyone knows what they're up to, though. She sez some of 'em are pushin' fifty, although it's hard to tell with all the heroin they take. Hard life, innit? Ya can see it on their faces. They hang about ger-rin pissed in Vicky Centre bus station in the afternoons, so Smanfa makes us get the 45 on Sat'days coz it drops ya off at Broadmarsh instead.

They don't say, "Are ya lookin'?" when ya go cot-tagin'. They'll be like, "What ya doin' knockin' about in here then, lad?" or "What ya on wi'?" or summat daft like that, but what they really mean is "I'll gi' ya ten quid if ya come an' suck ma cock in that cubicle." It's different for lads. Not that I'd do it for that price, mind. I'm worth at least fifteen. A pound for every year, plus one for luck. Twenty if yer lucky. I gorra tenner that first time, but I've learned how much ya can charge since then. Can't go sellin' mysen short now, eh?

I like a bit of a flirt with 'em, but sometimes I wish they'd just come straight out with it. Sometimes they do: "I'll gi' ya fifteen quid to suck ma cock." Who said romance were dead? But if they go, "Yer gonna suck ma cock then, lad?" ya have to go, "What's in it for me?" which means, "How much are ya offerin' me?" An' then they'll go, "How much d'ya want?" an' then I'll be like, "Why don't ya make me an offer I can't refuse?" which is all good fun, but then they'll make me an offer I can refuse an' hurt ma feelin's. They don't call me soft lad for nowt.

They all like me, though. Reckon I'm good-lookin'. I get loads of attention. No one at school thinks I'm good-lookin', or at least they won't admit it. Coz I'm gay! Poofter! Bent as a nine-bob note! Shirt-lifter! Fudge-packer! Arse-bandit! Bender! Oh yeah, an' how could I forget – I talk like a girl, don't I? They go on an' on about it, they just never leave me alone. Why d'ya talk like that? Why d'ya walk like that? Are ya gay? D'ya take it up the arse? What's wrong wi' ya? It's not a comprehensive school, it's the Spanish fuckin' Inquisition. To be fair, they've bin callin' me a rent boy for years, an' now I am. Jamie Draper said it to me an' Miss Kinder made 'im apologize, but she wun't tell me worrit meant. I had to ask Smanfa to ask 'er aunty. Smanfa reckons I'm good-lookin'. She never feels beautiful, an' I think that's dead sad. Like, ya don't have to feel beautiful all the time, but everyone should feel it sometimes. Don't ya think?

I always look in the mirror before I leave the house an' tell mysen that I am be-yoo-tea-full. I saw it on this programme once called *Abigail's Party*. It's from like Old Mother 'ubbard's time, but the woman in it's just like me mam, tryna give people olives an' that. I don't think I've ever actually had an olive, but it's just the sorta thing me mam would like coz it's what posh people eat, innit? I bet Joan Collins has had one. An' that's what they have at this party. I reckon it does ya good to tell yersen yer beautiful. Gorra believe in yersen an' that. Coz if ya don't, no other fucker will. A lotta the attention I get in here though is coz I'm young, I know that. I'm not stupid. They love that. One of 'em sez I'll be too old in a few years, when I start gerrin a snail trail. I don't wanna be hairy. I like bein' smooth. I already shave ma legs, although there's not many hairs yet. I know boys aren't s'posed to, but I just don't like it.

There were someone quite unusual in there today, though. He asked me to pull ma pants down an' show 'im ma private parts. I'd never seen 'im before. Sez 'is name's Winston. Black man. Dreadlocks. Stands out like a sore thumb round here. But he din't wanna do anythin' wi' me, he just wanted to see worrav got. I thought he din't like me at first, I wondered what I'd done wrong. But he sez he's workin' on behalf of 'is "client", someone who's lookin' for a lad like me, apparently. A client "willin' to pay a pretty penny for a pretty boy". Sez I've bin wastin' mysen for pocket money round here, but I've struck lucky now. Coz Winston's gonna help me make some proper cash.

A LITTLE BIT OF LUCK

Winston wanted me to meet 'is mate. He's called Max. I had to go to Titchfield Park after school, he said they'd be in a white car, a sporty one like ma dad's. I got in the back an' could only see the back of 'is neck to start off with. He were wearin' joggin' bottoms an' had 'is 'ead shaved. Proper rude boy, proper Ali G. An' yes, I definitely would. You'd never know he were gay. To be honest, he din't talk much an' I cun' really see 'is face properly, but I kept catchin' glimpses of 'im in the mirror – an' he's gorgeous. I were fascinated by 'im. I love that word. It's like a good way of sayin' obsessed. Ya could say I'm *fascinated* by it.

I were dead nervous. I'd never done owt like that. All the pretty girls at school do stuff like that all the time, but I've never gone racin' wi' big lads. In fact, I've only ever bin in Gaz's car, an' Aunty Ray's. I din't even realize I'd wanted to go racin' till I got in with 'em. Not that they took me anywhere, mind. We just talked. I can't even remember what they said apart from ey up an' what the plan was. I really wanted 'em to just drive me away, just rev up the engine an' piss off somewhere. I'd have let 'em take me anywhere. But I agreed to meet this Max on Sat'day at midday in 'ucknall Market bogs. How's that for a date?

It were empty when I got there, but I din't care coz I knew I were movin' on to better things. I were washin' ma hands so din't realize he were behind me at first – he just come up an' put 'is arms round ma waist an' went, "*Hello, you*", like I were someone good or summat. No one's ever said *Hello you* like that to me. I turned around an' saw 'im properly for the first time, an' I've never met anyone wi' such blue eyes! He's got 'is left eyebrow shaved an' it looks dead good coz they're dead thick an' masculine. He's gorrit pierced, like Scary Spice. He's gorra bit of a goofy smile, but it's proper cute. Proper laddish. An' he's not an old man! Sez he'll be twenty-one soon.

He held ma hand as we walked to the bus stop so I were like, "Ya'd better not do that round here." I din't let go, though. It were weird, I just kind of feel like I don't care about anythin' when I'm with 'im. It's not like anyone's gonna beat me up when we're together, is it? He's like proper grown up. An' they beat me up anyway, so what's the point of pretendin' yer not gay if yer already gerrin gay-bashed? Might as well be hanged for a poof as for a lamb.

I've never bin to a hotel before. Well, not a posh one. It's called the Hilton. Max sez it's gorra swimmin' pool. Gaz took me to a yoof hostel in the Lake District once, but that's about it, really. I follow Max up to the room an' he introduces me to the bloke. Sez 'is name's Dave. I'm thinkin', Yeah, an' I'm Joan Collins. They always lie about their names. I mean, I do too actually coz I don't want 'em knowin' ma real name. It's just what ya do. I go, "Hi, I'm Nick." Like Smanfa's brother.

Well, this Dave's disgustin'. Fat an' old an' hairy. He wanted me to kiss 'im, but I just cun' do it. It were too much. He's older than Gaz, for God's sake! An' 'is breath stinks. He must like bein' with us though coz he keeps cummin' an' cummin'. Dirty old man. I din't wanna suck it at first coz it were all slimy, an' I've never seen one like that, but Max sez, "That's just precum, don't be rude", as if we're in *Pride an' fuckin' Prejudice* an' I've just made some awful faux pas by askin' the wrong person to dance. I thought, *Rude?* Is he serious?

So that's where I'm sleepin' tonight. Old Mother 'ubbard thinks I'm stayin' wi' Gaz, Gaz thinks I'm stayin' wi' me mam, an' me mam thinks I'm stayin' with Old Mother 'ubbard. They'll not check or nowt. Clever, aren't I?

Dave's leavin' dead early. It's like five o'clock in the mornin'. I've hardly slept. We've bin waitin' for 'im to go for ages. I like this Max. Like, *really* like 'im. An' he likes me too, I can just tell. I reckon he's bin wantin' dirty old Dave to leave as much as I do, although he's bin actin' dead cheerful, like this is all totally normal. I'm half asleep an' waitin' for Dave to shut the door when we finally hear it go an' Max puts 'is arms around me. It's still dark outside but I can hear people startin' to move about. Bin men. Buses. The smell of breakfast comin' down the corridor. An' I'm so happy, coz I'm here, where I'm not s'posed to be, an' it feels amazin'. Just me an' Max, together. An' we've done it! We're rich! Well, by ma standards.

He jumps up an' sez he needs a wee, but I can't hear anythin'. The toilet door's open an' lettin' light in. He guz, "It's hard to piss with a semi", so I go in. I don't wanna spend a second away from 'im. The light hurts ma eyes, but I don't care coz it's just us. I feel like Bonnie an' Clyde or summat. I s'pose it is illegal, what we've done. I love misbehavin'. It's the best feelin' in the world. Well, maybe second best coz then Max is kissin' me an' it's like a dream. He drags me back to the bed an' guz, "Come an' 'ave a look at this." An' there it is, one hundred an' twenty pounds! All for me. A hundred pounds is a lotta money, innit? Money don't grow on trees! It grows on dirty old men wi' greasy little dicks.

We get back under the covers. I've done things wi' quite a few people now, but I've never had ma chest pressed against someone else like this. He sez he don't mind ma scar, reckons it's quite cute, actually – unique, like me! I'd never really thought of it like that before. I've gorra skin graft from when I pulled a pan o' boilin' hot water on mysen when I worra baby. No one's seen it coz I've always bin in cars or cubicles an' places like that. 'Is chest's broader than mine. I wonder if I'll end up as big as 'im? I hope not. I like bein' smaller, although I am big for ma age. I'm taller than Gaz now. Max's got lovely legs too, dead muscular like David Beckham. An' he's got hair in all the right places. In fact, I just love everythin' about 'im.

He puts the radio on. 96 Trent FM. They're playin' dance. *Love, life and laughter, is all I believe.* Dreamer. Ma favourite. How can I explain it? I just feel . . . warm. An' safe. *Here we lie all alone, am I dreaming?* He gets me on ma back, an' kisses me. *Your heart's smooth, my soul is unbelieving.* Sez he wants to go inside. *Now you see the me and I'm feeling, I'm feeling.* We just stare into each other's eyes. *I feel your hands, your lips, the heat of your body,* an' he looks at me an' guz, "I love ya." *Whisper your love to me say that you love me.* As he sez it, I realize I love 'im, too. *Please just love me down and never leave me.* I wanted ma first time to be special, an' this is it. *I'm a dreamer.*

It hurts, but I want 'im to like me. I think he's pleased

wi' me, an' I like how close we feel. I start thinkin', This is about as close as ya can be wi' someone else, innit? 'Is 'ead touchin' mine, 'is body inside ma body. It's amazin'. An' for a minute, it's like all I can feel is 'im. The whole world just dissolves into blackness, like on *The Never-Endin' Story*, till nowt else exists. There's just us. Me, Max, an' the feelin' of 'im between ma legs.

Well, I weren't expectin' any o' this. I've never let anyone do that to me before. But he loves me! An' I love 'im! Although part of me thinks guys like Max might just say stuff like that so you'll have sex with 'em. But he could love me. I reckon I'm the sorta person ya either love or hate, but I'd rather that than be borin' like most people. People are always tellin' me I'm "a one". I don't really know worrit means but it must be like "one in a million", although everyone's one in a million if ya think about it.

Now he's takin' me for breakfast in a greasy spoon. I'm clearly livin' in an alternate universe, where normal rules don't apply an' I can do whatever I want. No Gaz tellin' me what to do, or how stupid I am. Max loves me. Somebody actually likes *me* for me! The thing is, Gaz reckons he knows who I am better than me, but Max accepts me as I am. There's some builders in the café so I can't hold 'is hand, but I'm startin' to feel like I cun' give a flyin' fuck what people like that think about me. So long as they don't beat me up, mind.

I'm not stupid. I know it's not how it's menna be. Yer not s'posed to have sex for money wi' the person ya love, are ya? It's not exactly *Romeo an' Juliet*, is it? But it feels good.

I've never bin to HMV this early. I've bought singles in 'ucknall – I've got "He Wasn't Man Enough For Me" by Toni Braxton on CD – but I've never bin able to afford an album. I'm gerrin one by Moby coz he's in all the adverts, an' one by Kelis wi' that song that guz, *I hate you so much right now*, coz I sing that about Gaz. An' I'm gerrin *Ray of Light* by Madonna coz Max sez it's got that song on it where she guz, *An' I feel*. Aunty Ray sez it sounds like she's goin' "Anna Friel" off of *Brookside*, like that time Mammar Joe thought that Bee Gees song were "Bald 'Eaded Woman" instead of "More Than A Woman". Silly old Mammar!

I really like the look o' this Madonna album. I thought she were Marilyn Monroe when I were little coz they had this old video of 'er on the telly where she were dressed like 'er, surrounded by all these men. She seemed to be havin' a good time. Then a few years later, I saw this woman wi' short black hair on TV an' I were like, "Mam, who's that?" an' she explained it were Madonna, an' that she changes all the time. She sez, "That's 'er thing." An' I liked that that were 'er thing, coz I wish it were ma thing too. Me mam's mate Denise used to have one of 'er albums on cassette an' it's got this song called "Vogue" where she sez it don't matter if you're black or white, if you're a boy or a girl, an' she wants everyone to dance with 'er. Well, I wanna go an' live wherever she is, coz round 'ucknall it's actually quite a big fuckin' deal if yer skin's a different colour, if yer a boy or a girl.

CAN'T GET YOU OUT
OF MY HEAD

People at school say they're in love all the time but I think that's ridiculous – as if ya can be in love at our age! I guess me mam were sixteen when she met Gaz. She were walkin' down the street wi' Denise an' he wolf-whistled 'er. He worra few years older. Not that that ended well. But I do think they were in love. I reckon he still loves 'er, actually. But this is different. Coz I *love* Max Loxley. Or should I say, I am *in* love with 'im. That's more grown up, innit? He din't wanna tell me 'is last name at first, but I seen it on 'is business card. Max Loxley. Sounds like summat outta Robin Hood, don't it! Max Loxley. I love just rollin' the sound round on the end of ma tongue. It's almost as good as the real thing.

How many people end up marryin' someone they met at fourteen, though? They're all stupid at school anyway. To be fair, most grown-ups are too. Like in the shops an' that, people talk absolute bollocks. Just pure, non-stop shite. I were in the newsagents the other day an' there worra picture of Victoria Beckham on the cover o' the *Sun* an' the woman in front of me guz, "Ooh, look at the state of Posh Spice", an' the bloke behind the counter went, "That's not Posh Spice, is it? She looks like an owd bleddy woman!" coz that's how they all talk round here, innit, an' I were thinkin', Oh just fuckin' shut up an' gimme ma chewin' gum, will ya?

So maybe I don't love Max. Even if I think I do. Which I definitely do. I think. It's just a little crush. Possibly an obsession. People say I get obsessed wi' stuff an' I reckon they might be on to summat when it comes to Max Loxley. I think about 'im on the way to school, an' I think about 'im on the way home. I think about 'im in lessons, an' I think about 'im at lunch. To be honest, I reckon the only time I'm not thinkin' about 'im is when *Big Brother*'s on. Gaz don't know about 'im, obviously. It's forbidden love! Like *Romeo an' Juliet*. We're doin' it in English at the moment an' we watched the film – the one wi' Leonardo DiCaprio – an' apparently they were about our age coz people got married at twelve back then, an' that's menna be one o' the greatest love stories ever, innit? So maybe ya can fall in love at our age. Oh, an' Leo DiCaprio! He's gorgeous! I definitely would. If I weren't in love wi' Max.

Max'd buy me fags if I asked 'im, but I don't need 'im to. I don't have problems gerrin served usually, although some of 'em can be a bit funny wi' ya. Thank God I'm tall. I can't get alcohol yet though, so that's where he does come in handy. I've started twaggin' off school an' goin' to meet 'im in the afternoons. He always buys me Bacardi Breezers from Tesco an' feels me up on the park. I've told 'im he's takin' advantage of me, although, to be honest, I'd let 'im take advantage of me all the time if I could. If he knew I felt like that though he could take advantage o' that too, eh? Knowledge is power, as they say. I like gerrin drunk, but it's time I started doin' it in style. I reckon I'd get in round Nottingham if I dressed up. Max has told me about this bar he guz to called AD2. Used to be called the Admiral Duncan. Apparently they play a lotta Steps coz it's a gay bar. An' ABBA, coz he reckons they love all that. He sez he can't take me, though, in case he gets me into trouble. I think he means in case *I* get *'im* into trouble, but whatever. I love Max, but I'll go by mysen if I have to.

I'm off to meet Max down Mansfield. I've got ma head-phones on. Madonna. "Music". I'm worried I might look a bit gay. But I'm already on the bus now so there's not much I can do about it. I'm wearin' ma Adidas T-shirt wi' the lime green stripes, an' ma Nike Air Max. I've started to care about ma underwear now people see it, so I'm wearin' the grey pants me mam got me from Marks an' Sparks. I've had to wear a belt coz the Walkman makes ma combats fall down. I love 'em, though, I look like I'm in All Saints. I could do with a handbag, to be honest, but lads aren't allowed, are they? I've got ma hair in a quiff – a quiff! I love that word. I were gonna put on some coloured hair gel, but that really is too much for Mansfield. We could get gay-bashed if we're not careful!

They're proper mutants round Mansfield.

I do look dead cool, though. Everyone keeps tellin' me I'm gay so why shun't I look the part? When I got on I asked the driver, "D'ya go all the way?" an' we just burst out laughin'. To be fair, I did say it in a very sexual way. But that's just how I am. I don't fancy 'im. It's Hannah Bailey's dad! Funny though, aren't I? I'm determined not to lose ma ticket so I've put it in ma wallet. Smanfa always folds 'ers an' hides it behind 'er phone case, but I'd just end up losin' the whole phone if I did that. Mam got me a Nokia 3210 for Christmas an' ya can change the cover on it. It's the best Christmas present I've ever had. Before that, I'd have probably said it were Lego – ma pirate ship, or Robin Hood's castle. Burra love gerrin texts from Max.

I like bein' excited but sometimes I get too excited, d'ya know worra mean? It's like I can't keep still – I'm like a bagga beans! That's what Mrs Clarke used to call Wayne in English. No. Wait. Hang on. Worms. "You're like a great big bag of worms, you are, Wayne." That's what she used to say. Well, I'm like a great big bagga worms on this bus. I love buses! I always sit at the back. Everyone's dead bad on the way home from school, although I always behave mysen when I'm on ma own. I like lookin' at the parks an' old houses. Everythin' looks dead nice when yer just goin' past, don't ya think? I bet most places would be 'orrible if ya actually had to go an' live there, though. D'ya know what else I like lookin' at? Lads! But it's the same problem, coz most of 'em would be dead 'orrible if ya stopped an' talked to 'em. Not that I would, obviously. Most lads don't like me, although I reckon one or two at school do but are too scared to admit it. Like David Gammon. He definitely likes me. He's ma dream man. I mean, after Max. An' Jude Law. An' David Beckham. Oh, an' Craig from *Big Brother*. He's not even that good-lookin' really, but I just really like 'im.

I'm about to burst by the time we pull into Mansfield bus station, but Max in't where he said he'd be. We always meet at the same time an' place on Sat'days. I were gonna ask 'im if we could go an' see *The Beach* an' get ice cream, coz it's only a 15 an' I reckon I can get in with 'im. I don't have any credit though, so I've had to come to a phone box an' reverse the call coz I've got no change either. I've seen that on telly, ya dial up 100 for British Telecom an' the operator calls whoever it is ya wanna speak to an' asks 'em if they'll accept the charges. But she sez, "I'm sorry, it's going straight to his voicemail. Would you like to try again later?"

I've bin tryin' every fifteen minutes for the past two hours, but he's not pickin' up. He's nowhere to be seen.

THE BOMB

Mam's ruined everythin'. I hate 'er. I absolutely fuckin' hate 'er. I can't believe she's done this. I'll never, ever forgive 'er. She asked me if I were in love. I were dead shocked. I sez, "How the hell do you know?" She sez it's obvious – coz I'm always on ma phone, apparently. Always textin'. Always happy. Always gerrin excited every time it beeps. Like it's a crime! Well don't worry, coz Lisa's puttin' a stop to all that. She sez I've bin on a completely different planet for the past few months. Oh, she can be so clever. Not like Gaz. Well, she went through ma phone – *ma* phone, *ma* personal messages – an' then she went an' met Max. She actually met 'im! Face to face. Behind ma back. I can't believe it. Me mam! An' Max! Together!

How could she do this to me? How could she destroy what me an' Max have? Meetin' Max is the best thing that's ever happened to me. No one else treats me like a grown-up. Well, I'm sick of 'er, sick of Gaz, sick of everyone! Max is literally the only person who makes me happy an' she's gone an' ruined it. I'm livid. She's just as bad as Gaz, why has she done it? She guz, "Byron, yer fourteen years old – what d'ya expect me to do if I find out ya goin' out with a grown man? I'm yer mother, for God's sake." I'm like, "Oh, yer ma mother now, are ya? Coz you've

43

never bin to parents evenin', never thrown me a birthday party an' ya send me off to Mammar Joe's at the weekends so ya can go out clubbin' wi' Denise! An' the mam o' the year award guz to – *drumroll* – Shirley Valentine!" She slaps me. Hard. I run up to ma room an' cry.

He sez he can't see me no more. She told 'im she'd go to the police if he don't keep away from me. At first he tried to tell me he'd just bin thinkin' about our age gap an' realized it were wrong, but I'm not stupid. I knew he were lyin', so I got the truth out of 'im. An' it makes sense now coz the other week I were givin' 'er a cuddle an' I were wearin' aftershave an' she sez, "Have ya gorra girlfriend?" I sez no, so she sez, "Have ya gorra boy-friend?" An' I just laughed. She sez, "Ya can tell me, ya know, I don't mind." Well, if she don't mind why has she gone an' fuckin' ruined it? Just coz she's got bad taste in men, don't mean I do. Max is a nice person.

Well, Gaz is right about one thing, she's manipula-tive. I wish she'd just stayed in Turkey now. She told Max to be nice about it when he broke it off wi' me. Oh yeah, Mam, tell 'im to stick a knife in me, but nicely. He sez I've gorra wait, that he'll hold on for me, that maybe we can make a go o' things when I'm old enough. Obvi-ously I don't want 'im to get into trouble. I mean technically he's a paedophile, innee? But it's not really like that, coz I wanna be with 'im. It's different.

She's deleted 'is number from ma phone. I've got no way of contactin' 'im. I even tried ringin' that Winston, but the line were dead. Why in't he callin' me? I can't wait two years! He'll meet someone else an' forget all about me. An' worram I s'posed do till then? Go to school? I fuckin' hate it. She's literally ruined ma life. What the fuck am I gonna do? I'm gonna find 'im, that's what. An' persuade 'im to run away wi' me. I have to talk to 'im.

STARLIGHT

There's nearly two grand. He keeps it hidden in 'is waist-coat pocket. I can't even remember how I found it now, I think I were just goin' through 'is wardrobe an' I found this big wad of notes. It's mainly twennies, but there's loadsa fifties too an' they're ma favourite coz ya don't see 'em usually. Ya can fit quite a bit of money in a pocket, an' a burglar would never think to look in there. Credit where it's due, that's quite a good idea for Gaz. Mind you, I wun't wanna be a burglar in Gaz's house. Can ya imagine if ya got caught? It's bad enough bein' 'is child when ya an't even done owt wrong.

He sez he don't trust banks. I reckon it's coz it's money he got from sellin' fags he bought in France. I'm gonna be rich one day an' have a massive room full of gold that I can dive into like *DuckTales*. When I were little, me an' Old Mother 'ubbard went to Blackpool an' won open-the-box at bingo, which is where ya have to stick yer hand in a bagga keys an' pick the one that opens this box wi' loadsa money in it. Well I did it, I picked the right key an' we won! I dropped it at first, but I felt around for it again. Everyone clapped as I walked back to our table.

I thought it were gonna come in a big suitcase like what ya see on telly. I were dead shocked when the man just handed Mammar Joe this wad of rolled up notes. I were like, "I can't believe it. I've never won owt before!" Which made Mammar Joe laugh coz she sez, "Yer not even ten years old – I've had the flu for longer!" an' she probably has coz Mammar Joe always makes out she's unwell, although Mam sez she's a just hypochondriac an' smokes too much. It worra good holiday, although one night they cancelled the show we were gonna see coz Princess Diana had died. I were upset coz I liked Princess Diana. Me mam sez she only used to take me to McDonald's coz Princess Diana took William an' Harry. Everyone was upset really, except for Gaz, obviously. He don't have feelin's, does he, apart from anger. To be fair, he gave Mammar Joe the money for that holiday. So he's not all bad. We bought 'im a mug that said "I went to Blackpool and all I got was this stupid mug" with a picture of a bloke on it who looked a bit like 'im. I'm not sure he saw the funny side.

When ya get the notes out they're all bent an' ya have to gerrem the right way an' fold 'em back up again. Obviously I wait till he's out. He's told me he's got savin's coz he's always goin' on about how hard he works an' how he's takin' me on holiday or gerrin an extension on the house. I'd rather the extension, to be honest. I can't think of owt worse than havin' to go anywhere wi' Gaz. He were 'orrible to me in Whitby. But I doubt he's gonna notice twenty quid missin' when he's got so many, so I just took one. It's so bad that he'd never think I'd dare. But he owes me mam loadsa maintenance money that were menna be for me, so fuck 'im.

Ya can actually do a lot wi' twenty quid. Smanfa's

brother reckons that'll get me on the bus, in the club, an' some Bacardi Breezers down ma neck. An' I should have enough for some chips an' the bus home, wi' change left over, apparently. When I'm old I bet I'll look back an' go, "Remember the days when twenty pound got ya drunk, an' chips, an' the bus back, an' change left over?" An' people'll just laugh an' not believe me. Ya know, like how old farts go on about how ya could buy a house for a farthin' or whatever it was back in Olden Times. Mammar Joe's always goin' on about stuff like that, an' how "dear" everythin' is now. She remembers when it were shillin's an' tuppence. Tuppence! That's like four hundred year ago.

I'm gonna sneak out tonight. I hope Gaz shuts 'is bedroom door. He's like a prison warden. He woke up once when I were already halfway down the stairs an' I had to wait ten minutes till he started snorin' again. I'm in the attic so there's two lots of stairs, an' I'm tellin' ya, there's about three steps in the whole house that don't sound like a crypt door creakin' open in an old horror movie. I sneak out all the time an' go up the hill, though, so I know exactly where to put ma feet now without makin' too much noise. There's a real skill to it. I'm like a friggin' ballerina going down them stairs.

I like goin' out when the whole town's asleep. I sit on the electricity box an' look at the moon. Some lads have painted a nob on it wi' spunk comin' out of it. There's a poem:

> Hickory dickery dock
> A mouse ran up me cock

The clock struck two
I shot me goo
Hickory dickery dock

It's stupid, innit? But it makes me laugh, coz readin' graffiti – or writin' it – is about all there is to do round here. Which is why I've decided I fancy a little adventure.

FLAWLESS (GO TO THE CITY)

Smanfa were dead worried. I were like, "Babe, come on, how much trouble could I gerrin to really?" As soon as I said it though we just looked at each other an' burst out laughin' coz Mammar Joe always sez I could get mysen into trouble even if I were locked in a padded cell by mysen for five minutes. But I never *really* get into trouble, do I? Mrs Clarke sez I'm like water – I can escape almost anythin'. Includin', it now seems, the cobbled streets of old 'ucknall Town! I showed Smanfa ma outfit an' she were like, "Oh my God, what would yer mam say if she saw ya dressed like that?" So I sez, "She'd say 'Take that off – it's mine!'" Smanfa went, "What if she notices it's missin'?" I sez, "With all due respect, I cun' give a flyin' fuck, babe. I'm still furious with 'er."

It felt so good as we went past the sign for Bulwell. See ya later, 'ucknall! I'd never bin on that bus at night. I've bin down that big road that takes ya into Nottingham when Aunty Ray took me to the pantomime. But it's dead bright on the bus. Ya can see yer reflection in the windows when it's dark. I don't really like how I look though, so I pressed ma face to the glass an' looked out into the night instead. We passed the golf course an' I just wanted to get out an' find people, just walk around an' make new friends. Mind you, I'd probably get beaten up within five minutes but still, there's a whole world out there, an' I'm gonna explore it.

Mam likes goin' out. She guz down Black Orchid. She come home with a black eye once coz someone accidently punched 'er while they were dancin' inside a cage or summat an' everyone were off their 'eads. An' I wanna go an' dance inside a cage while everyone's off their 'eads, although I don't know if they'll have one where I'm goin' an' I definitely don't need no more black eyes. This face has bin through enough. I mean obviously, when I first saw Mam's bruise, ma immediate reaction were "Gaz!" but she still laughs about it now, so she must have bin tellin' the truth. She hides a bagga speed inside 'er boots when she guz out so she don't have to carry a handbag – she thinks I can't hear 'er when she's on the phone to Denise!

She always comes home wi' loadsa phone numbers written on bits of paper an' throws 'em away the next day, an' I'm tellin' ya she enjoys that more than cleanin'. She got back at four o'clock in the mornin' once an' were dancin' round in the livin' room wi' no clothes on to the Prodigy! By 'ersen! I heard 'er tellin' Aunty Ray the next day coz she were worried she might have woken up Pop next door. But apparently he din't hear owt, which is good coz Pop's dead nice an' lets us take 'is rhubarb through the hole in the fence. He's gorra water fountain an' a pigeon shed too. He lets 'em fly over the field every day an' they come back to 'im. We've just got grass an' a broken fence that kids from school cut through so they don't have to go down the jitty. It pisses me off coz they wun't dare if Gaz lived here, but what can we do? The council's already replaced it twice. But they've got used to havin' the shortcut now an' jump over it till it breaks again. I hope they break their necks, the bastards. Gaz said he were gonna fix it but Mam went "that won't be happenin' any time soon, then." That were six months ago.

But this in't about them, it's about me. An' I did it! I snuck out, an' went to AD2. I just walked straight in an' ordered a Bacardi Breezer like it were the most natural thing in the world. An' they served me! Din't ask me for ID or nowt. I cun' believe it. I were shakin'. All them twats at school, they'll never believe I got served in town! I've always bin more grown up than them anyway. Especially the lads. I felt a bit sad, though, coz I've only ever got drunk wi' Max. An' I miss 'im. But I'm excited too. There's a disco ball hangin' from the ceilin' an' coloured lights flashin' across the dancefloor.

I decided to sit in the corner an' take ma jacket off. They were playin' "Rhythm o' the Night". They used to play that at the yoof house near me mam's, but I were always too scared to go in. It's lot more empty than I thought it'd be, but it is a weeknight, I s'pose. I'm wearin' me mam's favourite top. It's from FCUK. I like it coz it shows ma body off. I watched this programme when I were little an' they were makin' jokes about gay people listenin' to the Pet Shop Boys an' wearin' tight white T-shirts an' it just stuck in ma 'ead coz I liked the way it sounded. Tight. White. T-shirt. It's all the Ts, innit? Well, it turns out a lot of 'em do wear tight white T-shirts, actually, though not all of 'em. I don't think Max would. But I look good.

I were hopin' I'd see 'im. An' that he'd put 'is arms around me an' tell me he loves me. But he's nowhere to be seen – he's good at that. I don't stay on ma own for long, though. After five minutes this bloke comes over. I thought he were gonna ask me how old I am, but he guz, "Oh dear, we can't have a little chicken like you sitting on your own, can we?" An' I'm thinkin', Lil' chicken? What ya on about? But he offers to buy me a drink, like on TV. Sez 'is name's Peter. An' he seems quite posh, so I've not done too bad, have I? He's maybe mid-forties or summat. Around Mammar Joe's age. He sez, "What's your name?" but I don't tell 'im Byron, I tell 'im the new one. Not Nick. Ma favourite one. He guz, "Would you like to join us for a drink?" So I go over with 'im. There's about five or six of 'em. "Well," he guz, spreadin' 'is arms open. "Welcome to the Fallen Divas Project."

I've never met anyone like this lot. They're a right bunch, but I guess that's why they call us queer, innit? One of 'em's proper fit. Blond. Cute. Looks dead gay. Wears a denim bucket hat. 'Is proper name's Damian, but he sez everyone calls 'im Dirty D, an' so does Smanfa now coz I took a photo of 'im wi' ma disposable camera an' she thinks he's dead fit too. I don't think he fancies me though, he likes older lads. I'm a bit too girly for 'im. Well that's fine, coz he's a bit too girly for me. I'm a bit jealous of 'im, to be honest. I reckon a lotta folk who'd fancy me would fancy 'im. So I'm gonna keep an eye on 'im. Competition, innit?

There's this Asian one too. I din't even know ya could get that. There's only one Asian family in 'ucknall an' they run a corner shop. Talk about a stereotype. I tried to walk home wi' the lad once but he sez, "Ah'm the only Paki in 'ucknall an' yo're the only poof. We can't be seen together." So I sez, "Fine, fuck off!" But he had a point. I can just hear 'em all now goin', "Oh look, it's Paki an' poof, skippin' home to bum." Well, this one's wearin' a hat too — why are they all wearin' hats? Must be about nineteen. Sez 'is name's Pavash, "But everyone calls me Fag Ash, coz I smoke like a chimney", then sparks one up as if to hammer the point home. He takes a puff, holds it for a second, then blows smoke in ma face an' guz, "*And* I'm a massive fag!" then tips 'is head back an' starts cacklin'. I dunno what to say, so I just go "Ooh" like a twat. It were so embarrassin'.

Then this girl in great big platform trainers comes bombin' over an' shouts, "I'm sweatin' ma cunt off, I am", before bargin' into Damian. So Peter guz, "Nikki darling! What wonderfully vibrant language, but why don't you say hello to our new friend", an' turns to me. She's like, "Ey up, duck, ya sure yer old enough to be drinkin' that?" But this Damian elbows 'er in the ribs an' nods to where the bouncer's stood, no more than three feet away. Well, I must have turned a whiter shade of pale coz this Peter guz, "Don't mind them, it must be awfully overstimulating for you, first time in here." I'm like, "Is it that obvious it's ma first time?" But I'm happy coz no one in 'ucknall uses words like that. Peter sez it's called the Fallen Divas Project as he has a habit of collectin' waifs an' strays. I sez, "Am I waif or a stray then?" "Oh," he sez, lookin' me up an' down. "You're definitely more on the waif side o' things." I thought, Oh give over, ya silly old poof! But I reckon I could get used to all this overstimulation business.

So there it is. I've got proper grown-up mates downtown now. I'm goin' back out with 'em soon. I even know worram gonna wear. Ma Kangol shirt, ma nice jeans an' ma seventy-pound trainers what Old Mother 'ubbard got me out the catalogue. I'm gonna borrow me mam's contact lenses too. I wear 'em to school sometimes an' everyone freaks out coz they make me look like I've got cat's eyes. Teachers don't like it, but they can't say nuffin, coz there's no rules against 'em yet. Hannah Bailey has some that look like footballs. I were jealous at first but cat's eyes are better anyway. I'll be like Michelle Pfeiffer in *Batman Returns*.

When I were little I thought dogs were boys an' cats were girls. Ma great-grandma used to have a dog an' a cat, an' I thought they were goin' out with each other till Uncle Andy put me right. Uncle Andy is Mammar Joe's brother, so ma great-uncle, really. Uncle Andy an' Uncle Roger are alcoholics so if anyone ever buys Mammar Joe a bottle o' booze for Christmas she has to hide it under the kitchen sink behind the bleach in case they come round. It's a shame coz Uncle Roger's dead clever. When Mam were little he come round so drunk once that Mammar Joe had to put 'im in the coal shed. He woke up black.

Mam sez yer not s'posed to share contact lenses but fuck 'er, she's ruined ma life. Anyway, I wash 'em. Ya have to use this special liquid from Boots an' rub 'em between yer fingertips. Yer hands have gorra be dead clean. I love cleanin' things. I've got that off 'er. I'm gonna put ma hair in a quiff wi' Gaz's gel, an' glitter on ma cheeks. It's gonna be a proper little art project. I've gone down the yoof house near the leisure centre like that, but no one appreciates it round 'ucknall. They have a DJ booth, so you can play what you want, but no one likes ma favourite song so I always end up dancin' by mysen. I reckon gay people'll gerrit, though. They love that sorta thing, don't they? But Max in't like that. He don't even like clubbin', he reckons everyone's on drugs an' he's not into all that, although he smokes weed an' he's always got poppers on 'im. But I know he guz to karaoke night at AD2 on Sundays, coz he told me. That's where I'm gonna find 'im. I'm gonna surprise 'im.

I din't even know if it worra man or a woman at first. She were dancin' on a podium in NG1. I'd never seen anyone like 'er. I sez, "'Scuse me, I don't menna be rude but are you a man or a woman?" She just laughed an' went, "I don't know, duck." She had a bandana on an' a little top that showed off 'er belly bar. It had the Pepsi logo on it, but instead of Pepsi it said "Sexi". Sez 'er name's Lady Di. I go, "Like Princess Diana?" She sez, *Exactly*, darlin'. I'm a quintessential English rose, me." But I've never seen anyone so black in ma whole life. I guz, "What's yer real name?" She's like, "Deon. But no one calls me that. An' it's Lady *Die* – with an e. Coz everythin's better with an e!" I sez, "Oh, ma mammar's a 'Joe', with an e, like a man. But everyone calls 'er Old Mother 'ubbard." She sez, "Is yer mammar a transsexual?" I sez, "What's a transsexual?" She sez, "You'll soon find out if ya hang about in here, duck."

NG1's a gay club. It's an absolute freak show. An' I love it.

Peter sez Lady Die's androgynous. I love that word. He sez I am too, it's when ya look like a boy an' a girl at the same time. Sez I'm very glam rock, like David Bowie. Sounds good, don't it? Peter knows loadsa stuff like that. He sez I look "subversive" too. I can't remember what that one means, though. He really is like one o' them people ya see on telly, although he's a bit weird. He's got this collection of rubber toys from McDonald's coz he sez the smell turns 'im on. Lady Die sez it's a fetish an' he's a paedophile, but I don't think he is. He hangs about a place called the Jazz Café in Hockley. Sez I should come up some time, so I'm gonna go on Sat'day. It's just around the corner from Ice Nine.

Well, this Lady Die sez she knows Max too, an' that he's seein' someone else now. I sez, "Are ya 'avin' me on? We've only just split up!" But she definitely knows 'im coz she described 'is willy, an' she's right – it's like an air freshener canister. I knew this would happen. I knew it! An' it's all me mam's fault. I hate 'er. I s'pose I should just do what everyone else in 'ucknall does an' go an' find someone who knocks me about a bit, eh? Like I don't get enough o' that as it is. Well, this lad he's menna be seein's called Dalton an' she sez they always go down AD2 for karaoke on Sunday nights an' do "Islands In The Stream". Max is Kenny Rogers. It's like bein' punched in the stomach. Well, at least I know now. I'm gonna walk out if I see 'em. Guess I weren't that special after all, eh? How could I be so stupid? I lost ma fuckin' virginity to 'im! But I love 'im. I still love 'im.

Lady Die knows Fag Ash an' all. They go out together dressed up an' trick people. They're dead convincin', but obviously there's always some who can tell. I've told 'em ya can't fool all o' the people all o' the time, although I reckon I could. People can't tell if I'm a boy or a girl when I go out an' it makes me laugh coz I'm not tryna look like anyone really. I just wanna look like me. All night folk are comin' up to me goin', "Are ya a boy or a girl? Are ya a boy or a girl?" Even when I'm not wearin' makeup. It's coz of how I talk. To be fair, I've never seen anyone who looks like me – an' I don't think anyone else round here has either. Apart from Boy George an' that, but I'm on about in real life. I love the eighties. I reckon I were born twenty years too late. Mam always listens to Annie Lennox when she's cleanin', this album called *Diva* where she's wearin' loadsa makeup on the cover. She looks a bit like 'er.

Ma favourite outfit's this blue belly top Hannah Bailey left at Smanfa's – although she's always askin' for it in case Hannah comes round. It's a bit late though coz I've cut one o' the arms off to make it asymmetrical. Lady Die sez symmetry's borin', an' I agree. I wear it wi' me mam's cat collar, one I got from Ice Nine wi' studs on it, an' a chain I've nicked off the dog. I've gorra badge with a pair of lips on it an' a silver ring Peter gave me that I have to hide at home in case anyone asks where it's from. But the crownin' glory's ma hair. It's gerrin quite long an' I put it into spikes wi' this wax from Boots. One of ma earliest memories were walkin' by Trent Bridge with Aunty Ray an' lookin' up an' seein' this man wi' this massive Mohican. It were all multi-coloured, I cun' take ma eyes off it. I wanted to talk to 'im, but I were only little. I put coloured gel on mine. Peter sez it's a *look*.

I wear makeup too. It's funny how puttin' colours on yer face can make ya look better, innit? Ma favourite's eyeliner. I just love how it changes the way I look. Then

I draw black round ma lips an' fill in the middle wi' some green eye shadow Smanfa gave me from H&M. It makes me look dead pale, like Lord Byron. The finishin' touch is some glitter hearts from Claire's Accessories. Lady Die sez I look dramatic, an' I like that coz I din't know you could *look* dramatic, an' I am partial to a bit of drama. Gaz sez I'm an attention-seeker. Peter sez I'm a "kitchen-sink drama queen". I don't know what that means, but put it this way, I'm impossible to ignore. Everyone knows me, an' no one forgets meetin' me. Ya can see it in photos, people just gawpin' at me. I love it. I love bein' different. I am different. I'm special.

I get loadsa men after me too. We never pay for drinks. It's funny, coz gay guys say I'm too girly, but there's all these Persian guys that go down NG1 an' they love me. I don't really know if they're gay or straight, but they fancy us. Lady Die's bin with a few of 'em. One of 'em's dead cute, he always dances wi' me an' buys me drinks. There's actually summat quite nice about the fact he don't speak much English. I lie about ma age sometimes coz a lotta guys won't sleep wi' me otherwise. But some of 'em don't give a shit. I were sittin' at the bus stop on ma own last week an' this taxi driver rolled 'is window down an' guz, "D'ya wanna lift?" I don't know if he thought I worra boy or a girl, but he must've known I'm underage. Right outside Vicky Centre. That's like Gaz or Uncle John just chattin' up a fourteen-year-old in the middle of town! What if I'd have got in? What if I'd had sex with 'im an' then told the police? Peter sez there's cameras everywhere these days. I just can't get ma 'ead round it.

Not that I'd ever grass anyone up. I like goin' out, so I'm not tellin' anyone anythin'. Fuck that. I've thought about phonin' social services on Gaz before an' sayin' he's touched me up. I wish he would sometimes, coz everyone makes excuses for 'im now, but no one could defend that, could they? An' then I wun't have to live with 'im any more. I don't have the guts though. They might not believe me an' lock me up instead. An' anyway, it'd be wrong. I don't really wanna upset me mam or Mammar Rita like that, even though they do ma friggin' 'ead in. But I just I hate livin' with 'im so much. I hate bein' in that house. As soon as I'm old enough, I'm movin' out. Then I can do worra want.

Damian text me. "Sneak out 2nite. Every1s goin Palais.
C u ltr." Its proper name's the *Palais de Danse*. That's
French for "Place Where Everyone Gets Off Their Tits",
accordin' to Peter. It sounds quite posh though, so I
thought I'd better do ma makeup like Joan Collins. An'
guess who was out? Lady Die. Proper shockin' out to
Missy Elliott. I sez, "I wish I could dance like you an'
Fag Ash", an' she turned round an' went, "Me black as
tar an' gay as a goose, darlin' – if I cun' dance there'd be
summat seriously wrong wi' me." Although there's summat seriously wrong with all of us, if ya ask me. I reckon
Lady Die's ma best mate now. Well, along wi' Smanfa. I
call 'er a stupid black bitch sometimes. She calls me a
stupid white slag. She knows I don't mean it, though.
She knows I'm not racist.

Pavash calls 'ersen Asha when she's dressed up. When
she looks good, she looks like Princess Jasmine. On a
bad day it's more like Jafar. She hates people sayin' that
though, an' by "people" I mean "me". I've told everyone
at school I won't answer to Byron any more. Hannah
Bailey shouted it from across the road on 'ucknall High
Street the other day – I think she wants 'er top back – an'
I just carried on walkin' an' made out I cun' hear 'er. The
Fallen Divas only know me by ma new name, although

Dirty D knows ma real name coz 'is next-door neighbour's sister went to school wi' someone whose best mate used to do me mam's hair. But I've made 'im promise on 'is mam's life not to say owt. He gave me a pill. I were worried coz I don't wanna end up like Leah Betts, but they've all had 'em before, so I thought, Fuck it, why not? Everyone else does 'em.

I sez, "Ooh, Dirty D! Ya do live up to yer name, don't ya?" although I cun' really tell if it had done owt to me at first. But after the club we all ended up goin' back to his. Fag Ash went off wi' some lads. She just got into a car with 'em – four lads, an' she din't even know 'em, so maybe they've found out she's a man an' murdered 'er. She's lost 'er phone too, so I guess we'll just have to wait an' see if she's out next week. We gorra bus to Basford, but we had to walk to Dirty D's. They said it weren't gonna be that far, but it took aaaaaaaages.

There were me, Lady Die, Dirty D, Sticky Nikki an' this lesbian called Jo. We played truth or dare while we were waitin' for the bus, an' them lot dared me to run down Parliament Street naked, so I did! Right outside Boots in Vicky Centre! I'll do owt for a laugh, me, although I hate people who say stuff like that normally coz they're usually called Karen an' dead borin'. But I really will. Peter sez I've got no boundaries. I sez, "That's good, innit? No, no limits!" He sez that's one way of lookin' at it.

When we get through the door Damian guz, "Oi, look in the mirror, check out yer eyes," an' d'ya know, they were as big as the moon! They looked quite nice, actually.

I sez, "Why are they like that?" An' they reckon yer pupils dilate when yer on pills. It means you've "come up". I mean, I felt good, but not that different. I thought all the walls would be meltin' an' I'd be havin' mad hallucinations like what ya see on the telly, but it weren't really like that. We ended up havin' such a good time, though.

Me an' Sticky Nikki pretended to get married. We had a proper ceremony an' everythin'. We pulled down the net curtains an' I made them into a veil, Sticky Nikki were the groom an' I were the bride, obviously. Dirty D said I had no business wearin' white, so I sez, "That's perfect, babe, coz these net curtains are anythin' but." He were the vicar, an' this Jo gave me away. Lady Die made a big show of cryin' coz she sez that's what people do at weddin's. We reckon it would've bin legal in Olden Times.

I do think those pills sent us a bit funny though. We were tryna climb inside the washin' machine at one point coz Sticky Nikki were convinced it worra portal to another universe, daft bogger. But ya never know, do ya? We were just bein' silly. We all get a bit carried away when we're together. Jo don't do owt like that though coz she sez 'er dad took too much LSD in the seventies an' now he's a bit antisocial. I guess ya do have to be careful wi' these things.

God knows how we din't wake up Dirty D's mam an' dad. They're dead nice, they know he's gay an' they're not even bothered! They don't even mind 'im havin' gay people round. When I woke up it were dead late an' everyone were in the back garden listenin' to Kylie Minogue. 'Is mam an' dad must be loaded coz they've gorra table an' chairs for the garden like Mammar Rita, an' a patio to put 'em on. They were all laughin' coz Lady Die were singin' the Spice Girls – "2 Become 1" – but instead of, *Set your spirit free*, she were goin', "Ya've bin fuckin' me, an' ya gave me HIV." We're gonna form a band wi' Fag Ash, although I can't sing an' I don't really like Fag Ash, to be honest, but we need three to make it like Destiny's Child.

Dirty D reckoned we were still a bit "up" from the pills coz we were in such a good mood, so I sez, "What shall we do then?" So Die's like, "It's a nice day, why don't we go for a walk?" An' I'm thinkin', I know, why don't we go to Newstead Abbey? Gaz used to take me there after Sunday dinner at Mammar Rita's. She lives in Linby, this dead nice village next to 'ucknall, an' ya can get to it from there. It's a lovely walk through all these fields an' woods wi' streams runnin' through 'em. I don't know where ya get the bus to Linby though, or if there even is one coz it's dead tiny, so I sez, "We'll have to go from mine." I thought, Fuck it, I'm takin' the Fallen Divas Project to 'ucknall.

ANOTHER CHANCE

Nikki said she needed to nip home an' put 'er trainers on so we all piled round there first. She's gorra van restin' on bricks on 'er front lawn wi' no wheels on it, so we went an' sat in that. Then 'er mam come out in 'er dressin' gown an' guz, "Ey up, d'ya wanna cuppa tea?" Dirty D asked 'er if he could have "twos" on 'er fag – an' I'm thinkin', Oh my God, did ya really just ask someone's mam for twos? But she guz, "Course ya can, duckie!" Me mam would never share a cigarette wi' me, she'd go mad if I even asked 'er. An' she don't call 'em fags, either. She sez that's common. Well, this tea makes us "come up" again, so we were all feelin' perky by the time we got the bus. An' I were worried what folk might say, coz ya don't get gay people round 'ucknall an' ya can tell by the way Damian walks, an' Lady Die is just – well, she may as well be from another planet. I sez, "Look, try an' tone it down when we walk through 'ucknall, OK? No prancin' about." But I'm thinkin', Fuckin' hell, I sound like Gaz. That's worram always in trouble for, ma mannerisms. But I'm not embarrassed by the Fallen Divas. I just don't want anyone to start on 'em. Or me, if I'm honest. Coz I still have to live here, for now.

We got off at the market. Picture it. Me, Jo, Sticky Nikki, Dirty D an' Lady Die, lookin' like a pack of space bunnies descendin' from the mothership – 'ucknall din't know what had hit it. Lady Die were drawin' the most attention. She sez, "Have they never seen a black person before?" coz people were starin' at 'er, but truth told I'm not entirely sure everyone round here has. She were like, "I can't be doin' with it", which she sez all the time. I've started sayin' it too now coz ya end up talkin' like people when ya hang about with 'em. I felt bad coz I know what it's like round here, but it were alright coz we got to Gaz's before anyone chased us away wi' pitchforks or owt. I made 'em wait round the corner while I checked Gaz weren't in. It helped that Nikki an' Jo were there coz Jo has long hair an' ya can't tell she bats for the other team on the rare occasions she's not runnin' around screamin' "I'm a dirty lesbian", but he were out anyway. I put ma scruffy trainers on an' we set off.

It worra beautiful day. Dead warm, but with a nice breeze. Newstead Abbey's miles away – it takes over an hour to get there – but as we got close we come to this dead nice field with all flowers in it. So like a meadow, innit? An' it's just lovely. Proper English countryside kinda thing. Mammar Rita would say it's "picturesque", coz that's how she always describes the Lake District. Nikki guz, "Let's have a break an' I'll build us a dirty spliff", so we flatten out a little patch an' lay our jackets down. I've never heard anyone call a spliff dirty before. It reminds me of when I were little an' Mammar Joe said she needed a "strong cup of tea" an' I din't understand how tea could be strong. Me an' Lady Die are puttin' on posh voices an' "givin' everyone joke", as she puts it. She keeps callin' me Lady Battenberg an' goin', "My dear Lady Battenberg, can I interest you in this exceedingly good cannabis cigarette?" So then I'm like, "My dear Lady Die, I would be very happy indeed to take you up on this most kind offer."

It were strange coz when ya take drugs in a club, ya feel like yer doin' summat wrong. But this were different. It just felt . . . pure? Like, OK, we might have bin off our 'eads, but Sticky Nikki sez weed's natural anyway coz it's a plant an' hippies smoke it. She reckons that's why they hug trees an' that. I just remember lookin' up at the sky an' tryna work out shapes from the clouds, like they do in films. Obviously me an' Lady Die just saw loads of cocks, so she guz, "It's cloud cock-o land up there", an' we all just burst out laughin'. I went dead dizzy after that. The nice way. The grass hid us from the path an' we all just leaned on each other's laps, right there, in the field. An' then, well, I don't remember.

God knows how long we were asleep for. Maybe half an hour. Maybe ten minutes. I don't know who dropped off first, but we all drifted off in the end. I woke up feelin' so refreshed an' happy. Can ya imagine if someone had come by an' seen us? I mean, we weren't doin' owt wrong really, but we must have looked like a right bunch o' freaks. I can't believe I did summat like that. I don't even feel safe walkin' down the street in 'ucknall, but I actually felt relaxed enough to fall asleep in public. I mean, it were hardly Vicky Centre bus station. But even so.

They all loved the Abbey, especially the Japanese

water gardens. I were dead proud coz it were ma idea, weren't it? I only take people I really like there. The Abbey were torn down in Henry the Eighth's time, so all that's left's the facade. It's dead eerie. There's a stately home next to it where Lord Byron used to live, an' a lake with a tunnel runnin' under it to a boathouse. But the best bit's this waterfall ya can go behind. The grounds are surrounded by the most beautiful woods an' countryside you've ever seen. I want ma ashes to be scattered here when I die. There's a photo of me an' Gaz here when I worra toddler, in the gardens. He must have bin about twenty-two – so not much older than Nikki, really. It's the only photo of me an' 'im I like. It were sunny that day too, an' I remember feelin' safe coz Gaz is big an' strong. I remember everythin' from when I were little. I can go quite far back, I can even remember Aunty Ray pushin' me round in a pram once at Christmas an' lookin' up at the stars. An' I remember how Gaz were wi' me before he realized I am the way I am.

We walked back through an avenue of trees, an' it reminded me of a book I've got by Sir Arthur Conan Doyle where they're floatin' down this river in the jungle an' he sez the trees rise up to form a "majestic canopy". The branches were swayin' an' the fields looked hazy in the evenin' breeze. It were still hot when we got back, although it were dark by then. Everyone were dead hungry so I sez, "Why don't we make some food?", coz I bet Gaz's gone round Paddy's, but for once I don't even care coz what can he say really? That they've gorra leave? We an't done nowt wrong. An' if I'm makin' dinner, he can't really complain, can he? So I made spaghetti bolognese coz a) I know how to, b) I knew it would feed all of us an' c) it's ma favourite. It were also the only thing we had ingredients for.

Well, everyone starts joinin' in, don't they? Helpin' me chop onions an' grate cheese an' that. It felt like we were in *Friends* or summat. I tried to explain to Lady Die but she sez, "Yo're not wired up right, yo're not." Gaz did come back in the end, but he were fine. He put 'is 'ead round an' asked what we were up to. I sez, "We're makin' spaghetti bolognese, d'ya want some?" Everyone went quiet, coz I've told 'em about 'im, but it looks like I made it up now coz he were fine an' just took 'is in the front room. I don't think he knew they were gay, an' even if he did it's not illegal, is it? Actually – is it? No. Not nowadays. I don't think so anyway. No, coz how could they have gay bars? An' they'd have locked up Graham Norton by now. He din't say ma name in front of 'em, thank God. It cun' have gone any better really.

Who knew we'd end up doin' all that? But it made me sad too, coz I wish Max'd bin there. An' I wished every day could be like this. Maybe things not be so bad when I grow up. Maybe Gaz'll be forced to treat me wi' respect. Not that he treats anyone wi' that much respect, but at least he can't keep tellin' me what to do when I'm an adult, can he? An' ya don't get beaten up all the time when yer a grown-up. When we were cookin' it felt like . . . like everythin' were . . . how can I put it? Alright? I've had that a couple o' times. I remember bein' on the bus into town wi' me mam one time an' lookin' at rays of light castin' shapes on 'er jeans. We were on the top deck an' the sun were comin' in through the tree tops on 'ucknall Road. I could smell VO5 in 'er hair. An' I just felt like everythin' were gonna be OK. An' that's how I felt makin' spag bol. I'm worried, though, coz whenever I let myself feel like this, summat bad always happens.

GROOVEJET
(IF THIS AIN'T LOVE)

I've gorra boyfriend. I met 'im in AD2. We were stood outside havin' a fag an' I overheard 'is mate call 'im David so I sez, "Ooh that's a king's name, that is." He looks like Sting, an' he's quite good-lookin' for an older man so I've not done too bad, have I? I like 'im, but not like how I like Max. Lady Die don't go out wi' someone who looks famous though, so I've got one up on 'er, although she used to go out wi' this lad called Gareth who I really fancy, but he don't have a car like David. He's got loadsa money too. He's thirty-two. That's old, innit?

The only catch is, he's from Sheffield, an' they sound like proper mongs – although yer not s'posed to say that now, are ya? To be honest, I've never heard owt nice about Sheffield. An' I've seen for mysen now coz he took me to 'is house, an' I can confirm it's an absolute dump. Sheffield, that is. 'Is house is quite nice. They've gorra shoppin' centre called Meadowhall, but everyone calls it Meadow-*hell*, apparently. Lady Die sez she's bin shop-liftin' in there, so I sez, "Is there anywhere in the East Midlands that you *an't* bin shopliftin'?" She got caught nickin' from Poundland once.

David took me up to Manchester last weekend. He got us a hotel on Princess Street an' took me to Poptastic.

They have that in Nottingham too, but it's better up there coz it's bigger an' it's a different crowd. Everyone knows everyone down NG1. I wore ma red top. It's from a Halloween costume I made wi' Mammar Joe, but I've customized it an' put it wi' some black flares an' a bit of fake fur that Asha lent me round the waist. I took ma Polaroid camera an' David took pictures of me in ma underwear. He wun't let me take any of 'im though coz he's paranoid I'll get 'im into trouble. He made me wait in the car while he checked in. I look dead sexy in the pics.

We drove. He's gorra posh car an' wears trendy clothes an' always has nice aftershave on an' that. He's got good music too, he were playin' Café del Mar an' Ferry Corsten on the way up, an' he's lent me this tape wi' progressive house on it. He's like a proper man. Dead masculine an' strong. He had some coke an' kept puttin' 'is hand between ma legs. He pulled ma pants down an' played wi' me while he were drivin'! I sez, "What if a lorry passes an' sees?" But I liked the risk, actually.

I love bein' driven down country lanes at night. I just absolutely love it. It giz me this dead nice feelin', knowin' there's someone else in charge. That I'm safe. That I'm goin' somewhere. That I'm free. I looked out at the valleys an' all the little houses twinklin' in the dark, an' imagined the sorta people who lived there an' what their lives might be like. An' I just felt so happy.

To be honest, it's the only thing Gaz does that I like. Literally the only thing. He takes me for drives at night sometimes, just to get us out the house. He knows I love it when he sez, "D'ya wanna go fer a drive?" coz

I never say no. He takes me to the Showcase cinema. I prefer the drive to the film sometimes. If we get on a country lane or a quiet road wi' no cameras, he'll rev up just to scare me. He's not bothered about the speed limit. He's such an idiot. He loves windin' me up. I love it too actually, but only coz I trust 'is drivin'. Ma dad's a great driver. He's dead sure of 'issen on the road, ya just feel so safe. I don't know anyone who drives like 'im.

He spoils it sometimes though, like one time we were talkin' about what film we wanted to watch an' I wanted to see *The Princess Diaries* an' he were like, "What d'ya wanna watch that for? That's for bleedin' poofters!" I just get dead upset when he sez stuff like that, an' then he gets mad wi' me for bein' mardy, but I can't help it. I just go quiet an' then he'll go on about me bein' over-sensitive, so it's like a vicious circle an' I don't know how to make it stop. He sez I'm like a woman, that I can't let go of stuff. But he's right. I really feel things sometimes, an' find it hard to get back to normal. Coz it's just so unfair. No one else makes me feel like that. I'm always comfortable wi' Mammar Joe an' Aunty Ray. We might argue sometimes, but I know they love me an' they know I love them. But when Gaz upsets me, I just keep rollin' the words round in ma 'ead – like an obsession – an' it just stays there, fresh in ma mind.

Sometimes I think about openin' the door an' just jumpin' out. An' if it'd hurt. They roll when ya see 'em doin' it on the telly, an' I've never understood that. Coz the ground in't movin', so why should it hurt ya any more to jump out of a movin' car than one that's stood still?

No one knows where ya are when ya drive at night. They might know what road yer on or where yer goin', but when ma dad's drivin' me, only we know exactly where we are at that moment in time, an' I find that quite comfortin'. He takes me up to Newstead Abbey sometimes, an' ya go down all these long, dark roads. He stopped the car once, turned off all the lights an' got out to scare me. I were terrified. But deep down, part of me liked it. There's just summat exciting about the dark, in't there? Especially when it rains. Coz when ya go down those country lanes an' look behind ya, everythin' turns black. It's like nothin's there.

MUSIC SOUNDS BETTER
WITH YOU

Smanfa's bein' funny wi' me coz she don't like me takin' drugs. Feel like I'm fallin' out with everyone at the moment. She met me with 'er cousin Nicola down Notts the other day an' this Nicola were hungover so I sez, "Oh did ya have a good night?" An' she were like, "Yeah, I were completely off ma 'ead", so I were like, "Oh d'ya take drugs?" An' they both just looked at me like I'd accused 'em of murderin' someone. She were like, "No, Ah do not take drugs, thank you very much." So I were like, "Well, that's what off ya 'ead means", but they sez no it's not, it means yer drunk. But that's how we describe it. An' ma friends are a bit more educated than Nicola Langfield from fuckin' Bulwell.

Nicola's one thing, but why was Smanfa so offended? Coz that's like sayin' there's summat wrong with it, an' she knows I take drugs. She must look down 'er nose at me then. This is why I can't stand people round 'ucknall, they're so small-minded. Literally every single person I know takes drugs, but I'm not even allowed to ask Nicola the question. An' then, to top it all off, afterwards Smanfa were upset wi' me! Not only for askin' Nicola if she takes 'em, but for "admittin'" that I do! It's like, for God's sake, it's not illegal, is it? Well OK, that is, but ya know worra mean. An' I can't be doin' with it. I can't wait till I'm old enough to move out.

I've got mates who take drugs who've got great jobs an' better lives than anyone round here could dream of, so maybe Smanfa should get off 'er friggin' high horse, an' get high instead. Speakin' of jobs, Mam's got 'ersen a fancy job in an opticians now. She has to wear glasses to work to make people trust 'er, but they've got no lenses in 'em, it's just clear glass. She's bought trousers an' jackets. She's dead happy, coz she can go shoppin' all the time now. She used to clean toilets.

All Mam's bothered about is havin' nice things. Gaz sez she's up 'er own arse. Aunty Ray sez she's selfish. I've still not forgiven 'er. I'm talkin' to 'er, but it's not the same. She sez she were protectin' me from Max, but how come she's never protected me from Gaz? It's alright for 'im to pick on me an' make me feel like every single thing I do is wrong, but for Max to kiss me an' be nice to me, suddenly it's super-Mam to the rescue. Well she can fuck off! People are such hypocrites about sex. Gaz'd rather watch a man shoot someone than two men kissin' on TV. Wonder what he'd rather see in real life. I honestly think he'd prefer to see me kill someone than be gay. Maybe he will one day.

Mam's gorra boyfriend now too. Bobby. She works at the Station Hotel on Sundays – Smanfa's dad lives in there, apparently – but not coz she needs the money. She just likes bein' there an' figures she may as well get paid for it. So it's all Bobby this an' Bobby that now. I think this one might actually be serious, though. He's an IT technician. I were like, what? An' he owns 'is house. He's gorra daughter an' it sounds like she's dead spoiled. I think Mam's hopin' she will be too. It's nice that she gets 'er happy endin', I suppose. I, meanwhile, have had to dump David, coz he called Lady Die coloured. He come to pick me up from 'ers an' were like, "You look lovely, coloured folks always look good in bright colours." She just laughed, but I can't go out wi' someone that thick, canna? We all say stupid stuff, but come on. It's like the N-word. Everyone knows ya just can't say that if yer white, not even jokingly. I told this David that he shun't say anythin' in front of me that he wun't say in front of Natasha an' he starts goin', "I'm not racist", so we had this massive fall-out an' I thought, Oh fuck off, I don't even like ya anyway.

Natasha's ma brother's sister. She's mixed race. I call 'er ma sister, but we're not related by blood. She's not even ma step-sister. Basically, Gaz had a baby with 'er mam, so we share a brother. I call 'er every night, I know the number off by heart – 0115 9528920. She's dead pretty. She looks like Scary Spice. Sometimes we sing "Wannabe". I'm Ginger. Mam an' Denise see Natasha's mam Michelle down Black Orchid sometimes. Denise sez she cun' see 'er till she smiled. I laughed, but that's bad, innit? Denise sez, "What d'ya eat when ya go round Michelle's? Rice an' peas?" I din't understand that, but apparently that's bad too coz Michelle dropped me off at Mam's once an' as they were stood there talkin' I sez, "Michelle, Mam's mate Denise sez ya always eat rice an' peas, is that true?" Mam looked mortified.

They were the only black people in 'ucknall, although they've moved to Arnold now. I reckon Michelle wanted to get away from Gaz. I don't blame 'er, to be honest. Ma uncle John's wife is black too, but she's quite light-skinned. Someone called 'er a Paki walkin' down Annesley Road once. That's what people are like round here.

Natasha's the one who lent me 'er tights. School phoned Mam an' told 'er. I sat wearin' 'em, waitin' for 'er to come home. I knew she'd be upset. I must've bin about seven or eight. She told Gaz. When she went to Turkey, he took me to see the doctor about it, an' I told 'im. I'm a girl. I sez, "I've always known, it's ma earliest memory." I were on a bench – I must've bin about four – an' I told a girl, an' she shouted over to the lads on the swings, 'Oi, have ya heard what he's sayin'? He sez he's a girl." An' they all went, "Ah, that's naughty!" an' started laughin' at me.

The doctor referred me to a child psychologist, but Gaz never took me. I reckon he were worried what they'd say. Just think how different things might have bin if he'd taken me! If he'd believed me. But d'ya know what pisses me off the most? I don't think he din't take me coz he din't believe me. He din't take me coz he *did* believe me, an' he din't wanna face the truth. But the funny thing about the truth is, it always seems to come out in the end.

NEEDIN' U

Where the fuck is Peter? He said he'd be here half an hour ago, which also happens to be the exact amount of time since I smoked ma last fag. As in, the last one in the packet. Ma lucky fag. Whenever I open a new packet I always turn the one in the middle upside down an' smoke it last. It's menna be good luck, although it don't seem to have done much for me today. I've bin trapped inside the bogs at Nottingham train station for about forty-five minutes, an' I'm cold, knackered an' pissed off. I just don't see why it's takin' so long to get here from Arnold.

It all started in Birmingham New Street. Asha an' Lady Die wanted a coffee to perk up a bit. I really cun' face standin' there in last night's makeup an' a wig in the middle o' the afternoon, but they just don't care, do they? It were packed an' I just cun' be doin' with it. Asha looked the best. I hate 'er. She even brought a fuckin' bag wi' day things in it. Who the fuck brings an overnight bag on a night out? She put 'er hair in a ponytail an' popped on a cardigan an' actually looked quite normal-ish. Well, I still feel, an' look, like a piece of shit, hence why I'm hidin' in here. Thank God I had the sense to nick a coat from the club. There worra big pile of 'em on the floor on the way out, so I just took one. While we had a fag I put the hood up an' Lady Die sez I looked like the woman from the Scottish Widows advert. Fag Ash said I looked like Skeletor.

I were only gonna have a nap. I just wanted to lock the door an' feel safe. I can't cope without sleep. They can go all weekend, I don't know how they do it. I don't know how they could just fuckin' leave me there, either, but I woke up an' saw all these missed calls on ma mobile. I must've bin conked out for at least half an hour. I called 'em straight away, but they were already on the train back. How could they do that to me? I'd never treat them like that. Well, maybe Asha. But not Die. They know how much I hate the walk of shame at the best of times, let alone leavin' me to make ma way back from Birmingham all on ma fuckin' own. They don't understand, coz they don't have any shame. They were like, "We looked for ya! We called but ya din't answer! We thought yer'd gone off without us!" But why din't they knock or summat? Asha sez they could hardly have gone lookin' in cubicles, but if they really did give a shit about me, they could have waited. I can just see 'em now, Fag Ash nudgin' Lady Die an' sayin', "I know, let's just go without 'er!" wi' that grin on 'er face. That's just the sorta thing she'd do to me. I know it is, coz it's just the sorta thing I'd do to 'er.

Well, whatever. We had a wicked weekend an' so long as I get home, I don't really care. It's not like they don't disrespect me all the time anyway, is it? The thing that really pissed me off though is that I din't have any money to get home, an' we were s'posed to be skankin' the train together. Which meant I had to do it on ma own. An' it's a miracle I din't cringe to death. I thought I could just pretend to be asleep when the ticket man came, but the train were rammed. On a Sunday! People were havin' to stand. I managed to nab one o' them pull-down seats next to the bins, but there were loadsa people squashed round me. They must have bin able to see I were wearin' a wig, but I were just too weak to stand up.

When the man come I told 'im I needed to buy a ticket an' went into ma pocket knowin' fully well I had no money. I had to pretend I'd lost ma purse. It were so bad. It went dead quiet an' I could feel everyone lookin' down on me – metaphorically an' literally. I had about two pound fifteen, so only eight quid short! I must have looked so pathetic, coz he let me off, an' they never do that, especially not when there's loadsa people watchin'. Well, I won't be doin' that again, I can tell ya that for nowt. Guess we shun't have spent all our money on drugs really. An' it were ma idea to go out of town. I love bein' spontaneous, but the thing with adventures is, ya can't promise how they're gonna end. An' sometimes it's in tears.

Which is why Peter's comin' to rescue me. I reversed the charges. I sez, "Peter, I've got mysen into a bit of a pickle." He were like, "Oh, what a surprise!" an' starts goin' on about how I thrive in drama. I sez, "Look, I can't help it if I'm good in a crisis", so he guz, "The problem is, you sometimes go *days* without one." Oh, he thinks he's so clever. He'd better have the heatin' on in that car. I hate that Mini. I look ridiculous climbin' into a tiny little car wi' some weird old man behind the wheel.

God knows what people must think. Peter's older than I first realized. Reckon he's in 'is fifties. He's got records from the eighties an' that. Mam used to have a Whitney Houston record when I were little, but I've never seen one since. He's got "Tainted Love" by Soft Cell. He was actually there, in the hallowed decade.

He works at Jessops an' always has loadsa nice food from Marks an' Sparks in this fridge. He wears a hair-piece. It's basically a wig that's glued to 'is 'ead. I've no idea how. I daren't ask. He pencils in 'is eyebrows too an' uses fake tan. He's a bit silly really, but to be fair, he does look younger than he is. I reckon he's in love wi' me. He lives in Arnold, which he describes as a "cultural des-ert". I sez, "Move to 'ucknall an' see how ya like that, ya silly old poof." Peter's started buyin' me fish an' chips on Sundays an' givin' me an envelope wi' loadsa twennies in it. I don't even have to do owt with 'im most weeks. Where is he?

LOVE STORY

Them lot have started hangin' around wi' this lad called Liam. Proper fuckin' twat. We all went back to 'is the other night an' he kept kickin' me an' sayin', "No one falls asleep at ma parties, Tinkerbell." I'd told 'em I were tired, an' I must've bin coz I find it hard to sleep at the best of times an' they were blarin' out garage full blast. God knows why 'is neighbours din't call the police. Liam don't strike me as the sorta person who giz a flyin' fuck about 'is neighbours, or indeed anyone but 'issen, but I can't imagine he'd want the police round. He's growin' weed in 'is back room. Mind you, I don't think I'd dare call the police on 'im if I he were ma neighbour. Let's just say ya wun't wanna bump into 'im down a dark alleyway.

I'd left all ma stuff at Lady Die's, so I cun' have gone home without gerrin changed. She can go all weekend without rest, she's like a fuckin' Terminator. She made me feel like I were bein' unreasonable for wantin' to go to sleep. Like a, ya know, human bein'. She's the one I'm most upset wi' to be honest coz I din't think she'd like someone like this Liam. He's not a nice person. Not a nice person at all. So much for the Fallen Divas. I were thinkin', Ya don't kick a diva when they're down! But I din't say nowt coz Liam sez he hates "all that camp shit" an' takes the piss out of me whenever I try an' have a laugh an' that. Bastard.

They met 'im at Lost Weekend. It's a straight club, but it's pretty flexible. Die an' Fag Ash go all the time to this night called Lovezoo where they play funky house all night. There's usually a few bisexual guys in there – or there are by the time we're through with 'em. But it's about the music really, an' a common appreciation for mind-alterin' substances. Everyone gets proper battered. Well, Liam's one o' these who sez he's bisexual. Proper straight-actin'. Proper little bully. Hates pop music. Only loves R 'n' B an' all 'is mates are black. He don't like me coz I'm girly, an' white, so I'm failin' on all fronts as far as he's concerned. He's twenty-one an' got 'is own flat in Radford. I reckon he's a dealer. Either that or just a massive fuckhead – but he's never short of drugs, I know that. So obviously he's like the Piedfuckin' Piper to them lot.

I don't know why everyone seems to think he's so wonderful. Peter don't like 'im either, but Peter would never come to Lovezoo, he only feels safe in NG1. Liam don't go to NG1, he guz to the Bomb an' places like that. He kept playin' Layo & Bushwacka. I reckon he's in love. But it's dead catchy an' I can't help but think of 'im now whenever it comes on the radio. He knocks about wi' the Woodies – this big gang in Radford. They're at war wi' St Ann's. They've got guns. Even Gaz wun't mess wi' the Woodies.

I go in the kitchen an' he guz, "Get that down yer neck!" an' shoves this key up ma nose. I sez, "What do I want that for?" He guz, "Coz yer body don't produce Vitamin K naturally." I sez, "Ooh, yer tryna gimme that horse tranquillizer, are ya?" So he guz, "D'ya like horses? Coz I'm hung like one", but then he smirks at me, like the joke's on me an' I'm just stood there thinkin', Eh? Then Lady Die comes in an' shouts, "I dunno abaht you, Miss Ketamine, but I feel *so* much yummier!" an' morphs into Catwoman. Next thing I know I'm babblin' on about why are kettles called kettles an' ma arms are all long like Mr Tickle! It worra terrible way to carry on, really, but that's the youth of today for ya, innit?

You do feel cool hangin' round with 'im, but there's summat really mean about this Liam. It weren't just the way he kicked me. It were the fact he were laughin' at me, an' gerrin everyone else to join in with 'im. Lady Die were like, "Ah, leave 'er alone, Liam", but then she guz to me, "Don't go ter sleep, don't be mardy." An' I were shocked, coz I wun't just stand there if someone tried to humiliate 'er in front of me. I mean, she was rat-arsed, but even so. How could they like someone so nasty? The thing is though – an' I'd never admit this to anyone – but I really fancy this Liam. I don't think he'd ever look twice at me, though. I'm just dirt on 'is shoe. An' I don't gerrit. Coz Max would never treat me like that. An' I don't know how I ended up here, wi' someone so 'orrible. Or why I want 'im to like me so much.

By the time me an' Lady Die left it were mornin' so she guz, "Shall we get breakfast in McDonald's?" an' I'm like, "I din't even know ya could get breakfast in McDonald's." She must have bin feelin' guilty coz she were like, "Come on, duck, I'll get ya a bacon an' egg McMuffin", so I'm not as fucked off with 'er now, even though she insisted on takin' the bus back. I sez, "Yer havin' a laugh if ya think I'm gerrin on a bus dressed like this", but she were like, "If ya wanna waste yer money on a taxi, fine, but I'm not." It were light by then but I thought, Am I fuck payin' for a taxi if she's not chippin' in, so we got the 44. I've never bin out dressed like that in the day. I don't think I've ever felt so uncomfortable in ma entire life, an' that's sayin' summat. An' there weren't even anyone on it.

We had to climb over the fence when we got to 'ers an' I ended up gerrin all this green stuff on ma skirt. She said we had to go in the back way coz we look like prostitutes. I sez, "Die, we are prostitutes", but she were like, "Just coz I sucked someone off down a jitty don't make me a prostitute", so I were like, "Yeah, but it does make ya a fuckin' slag – at least I have summat to show for it." 'Er mam lives on a cul-de-sac though like Mammar Joe, an' she sez it's bad enough for 'em bein' the only black people round there, so I dropped it. But she is a prostitute anyway coz she stuck 'er finger up Sandwich-Van-Pete's bum an' sucked 'im off for fifty quid an' a line a coke in front of a room full of people at a house party last week, an' I'm sure it weren't the first time. For either of 'em. Well I've had ma last ham sandwich off of 'im, I can tell ya that for nuffin.

Anyway, I'm sat there takin' off ma makeup an' I real-ize I've lost ma fuckin' phone. Again! I knew I had it at Liam's coz I'd bin lookin' at the time an' feelin' annoyed at how late it were gerrin. An' I specifically remember it turnin' seven coz I told Die that if we din't leave within the next half hour we'd be goin' home when it were light, an' I really din't want that. An' I definitely don't remember havin' it in McDonald's. So I had to go back to Radford, an' see Liam. He made out he din't have it at first. Then he makes out he wants some money for lookin' after it for me. I sez, "Please stop messin' about." "Anyway," he guz. "How old are ya?" So I tell 'im. He guz, "When are ya sixteen?" I sez, "In a few months", an' ask 'im why he wants to know. He sez, "Here, take ma number in case ya ever need owt. K or owt like that."

MISSING

Lady Die bumped into Max the other day an' apparently were askin' after me. I'm pissed off coz she knows how much I wanna speak to 'im an' she din't get 'is new number, so I've made 'er promise on 'er mam's life that she'll gerrit if she sees 'im again. She guz, "I'm sure ya could find it on the back of any old toilet wall." Cheeky bitch. She sez he's always in town anyway coz he guz shopliftin' in Marks an' Sparks at lunch an' gets a chicken pasta salad for that bloke who's always sat outside H&M playin' a xylophone. She sez he takes orders, so she asked 'im to teef 'er some sushi. I've never had sushi, ya wun't even be able to get that in 'ucknall. So it's probably like totally delicious. I can't believe she din't get 'is number! She's a good laugh, but ya can't rely on 'er.

We were comin' back from Rock City the other night an' stopped to get some fags from the garage, an' these girls were stood behind us an' one of 'em went, "Fuck's sake, hurry up." Die sez, "Alright darlin', no need to be rude." An' the other one went, "That's a man. Look at 'em!" an' they both burst out laughin'. One black girl, one white girl. Like us, but the real thing. The black girl sucked 'er teeth an' was like, "Nah. Chi chi man." I don't usually argue when this happens – coz it happens every fuckin' time we go out – an' it's our own fault really, innit? I mean, we choose to come out dressed like this. We're askin' for it, really. But summat inside me snapped this time – coz it's so unfair. No one deserves to be treated like that. So we told 'em to fuck off, an' ran down the road.

Would ya rather have loadsa people hate ya an' loadsa people love ya, or not be hated by many people but also not be loved by that many people? People seem to have a strong reaction to me. Lady Die sez it's a hard question, but she'd probably rather be hated by loadsa people an' loved by loadsa people. Me too. Take the rough wi' the smooth. That's why I don't mind a comedown on a Sunday. It shows you've had a good night. In fact, I wun't wanna be doin' owt else on a Sunday other than layin' around feelin' like shit. I sez, "Die, d'ya think people are inherently bad or inherently good?" I like havin' conversations like that with 'er coz I don't have to explain what words like "inherently" mean. I sez summat were obscure once an' Dirty D were like, "You an' your big words, always showin' off." I sez, "How's that a big word? It's seven letters." People say "beautiful" all the time, an' that's nine. When people say "big word" what they really mean is "word I don't know". An' what other people don't know's not ma problem, is it? But I tell ya what, Dirty D sounds like Stephen Hawkin' compared to Asha. She really is thick.

I like a few hours to put ma makeup on an' that, but we can be ready in forty-five minutes if we have to – like a weapon o' mass destruction. Lady Die sez ma eye makeup looked feline the other week an' Asha were like,

"Ooh, feline – what's that?" so we told 'er an' later on she were goin' up to people in the loo sayin' "I like yer makeup, it looks dead *feline*." So the next time we were all gerrin ready I sez, "Ooh Die, what's that perfume yer wearin'? Ya smell proper faecal", an' winked at 'er. Well Asha's ears pricked up at that – talk about the dog takin' the bait – an' she went, "What's that?" I sez, "It means alluring. Like a mysterious air." Lady Die guz, "Yeah, *mysterious*! That's just the word." Asha guz, "Hmm, *faecal*. Fee. Cull. I like that. It's coz I'm wearin' Mysterious by Britney Spears." She spent the rest o' the night askin' strangers if she smelled faecal.

The Fallen Divas all talk like rude girls. Well, apart from Peter. An' Lady Die. In fact, she's the only one who sounds like a proper white person. Asha sez she's a coconut coz she's black on the outside an' white on the inside, although she does speak patois if she's tryna make us laugh, or when she's angry. Lady Die reckons people are mainly good. I don't know about that. Like look at that flood they've had in New Orleans. They were lootin' an' apparently people were rapin' people an' all sorts, coz people are evil when they think they can get away with it. It's why I worry about Mammar Joe. Ya read about old ladies who get attacked in their eighties an' that. Imagine thinkin' you'd made it through yer whole life without much bad happenin', an' then someone doin' that to ya. It must be 'orrible bein' a woman. I guess ya only know if you've made it through life OK just before ya die, but that's hardly gonna cheer ya up, is it? When yer on yer deathbed. I'm scared of dyin'. I don't wanna be alone.

Lady Die sez, "Right, I've got one. Would ya rather be rich, beautiful or clever?" She sez beautiful. Coz ya can use yer looks to get rich, or marry someone rich. I reckon ya need to be clever too though, coz there's loadsa pretty girls who are stupid an' have shit lives. But if yer clever, ya can work out how to make yersen rich, an' if yer rich, ya can pay to make yersen beautiful these days. But ya can't turn money into brains, an' ya can't turn beauty into money *without* brains, so it's gorra be brains. It's the only one that can get ya the other two.

Die sez "Money can't buy ya love, though." I sez, "Ya coulda told me that before I started sellin' mine." But it made me think about how there are some things no one can control. Coz it don't matter how rich, beautiful or clever ya are. Coz no one can protect 'emselves from dyin'. Anyone, anywhere could die at any minute. I could have foot an' mouth an' not even know! I could drop dead – right now – an' there's nowt anyone could do about it. Even Madonna. I find that both dead comfortin' an' dead scary.

After them girls called us men, me an' Die were saying how we'd love to do summat good one day, like be the first transsexual to have a number one, or be on the cover of *Vogue*. I reckon I will do summat like that ya know. God, can ya imagine? I could be the first transsexual on the moon! Like how ya get the first gay person to do summat, or the first black woman. I've never heard of anyone like us who's done owt good, but there's gorra be *some* out there who've got some talent. People always tell me I've got "potential". Lady Die's obsessed wi' Naomi Campbell an' sez I'm like Kate Moss an' we should go to London one day like Dick Whittington an' make our fortunes. That'd show everyone!

I don't think I could go to London. I reckon I'd get swallowed up in summat proper bad. I wanna go to make money, but Max used to tell me stories about the rent boys down there – an' they don't mess about by the sounds of it. He reckons they'll cut yer dick off if yer on their patch, not that I'd mind. He sez they're all on drugs. Proper drugs, heroin an' crack an' that, although I reckon he might have just bin tryna scare me. But no, there's too much temptation in London. I know worram like, I'd probably end up dead. That's what everyone sez when they see me: "Ey up, trouble." Coz I have this wonderful way of findin' it.

PASSION (DO YOU WANT
IT RIGHT NOW)

If Liam don't like me, why does he wanna be ma friend? He's 'orrible to me in front of other people. I can't work 'im out. It's like he likes me but don't like me at the same time – like maybe he's ashamed of me or summat. But he sez, "Why don't ya come round one night an' we can smoke a spliff." I sez, "I can't come out on a weeknight unless I stay out all night." I can't be bothered sneakin' back in. It's bad enough tryin' not to wake Gaz up on the way out. But Liam sez I can stay over. An' I just don't gerrit.

He used to live in Bulwell. Sez he knows Hannah Bailey's big brother, Simon, an' they used to look at porn an' wank off in front of each other. An' apparently this Simon don't even know he's bisexual! I said, "Is that normal? Is that what straight guys do together?" He were like, "Well, it's what we did." I just wish everyone at school knew coz Simon's menna be one o' the hardest lads in 'ucknall – an' he'd be the first to pick on me for bein' "bent as a nine bob note". If only they knew! When I told Liam that he sez, "Well, he were pretty hard last time I saw 'im", an' oh my God, what I'd have given to be a fly on the wall that day! Liam sez it's massive. I can imagine.

He had some pizza left over so we heated that up in 'is

95

microwave, but it din't fill me up so I went to the shop an' gorra treacle puddin' an' a tin of custard. That's ma favourite. I've gorra sweet tooth at the best of times, but I proper get the munchies when I'm stoned. He lives round the corner from Forest Road. The buildin' itself is nice, like proper Victorian, but it's dead rough round here an' I were in an' out o' the shop like a whippet. Weed makes me paranoid at the best of times, let alone round here. It's a massive house, but it's bin converted into bedsits now. I bet it would only have had one family in it when it were new. I'd love to buy a big house like this an' make it all nice again.

Liam's on the ground floor. I'd be scared on the ground floor if I lived on ma own in Radford, especially if I mixed wi' the sorta people he mixes with. There's a massive marble fireplace behind where 'is bed is, an if it's like ma dad's house, it'll have little fireplaces in the bedrooms an' all. I'd love that, to get 'em all workin' again. It can't be that much to get the chimney sorted out, can it? Just imagine how nice it'd be havin' a real fire in yer bedroom! Ya could sit an' read all night an' fall asleep in front of it. I did that in front o' the fire at Mammar Rita's once an' it's dead cosy. Imagine doin' it every night.

There's loadsa trees on Liam's street. It's one o' the things I like most about Nottingham, it's dead green. I s'pose they've done it on purpose coz people associate us wi' Robin Hood an' Sherwood Forest. It would've covered most of Nottingham back in Olden Times. There's a stone cross where Mammar Rita lives in Linby that's menna mark where the forest boundary were in medieval times, an' that's miles out. There were wild stags an' bandits roamin' about Nottingham back then. Now it's just drug dealers an' prostitutes.

I wash Liam's dishes up for 'im. I reckon that just about every pot, pan an' piece of cutlery is dirty so he's like, "Perfect time to do 'em then, eh?" I wanna ask 'im, "Liam, why did ya invite me?" but I daren't. I don't want 'im to tell me to leave. There's a police siren outside. He sez, "Oi, you've missed a knife" – an' pulls out a dagger. I'm like, "What ya got that for?" He sez, "Ah've gorra carry it, there's people after me. It's self-defence." I don't say nowt so he guz, "Ah can't help it, can Ah?" I go, "But ya wun't actually use it, would ya?" An' he's like, 'If Ah 'ad to Ah would." I sez, "Liam, ya could kill someone." But he sez it's not 'is fault, it's just the situation he's in. I can't help thinkin' it's Liam's fault he's in that situation – I mean, ma Aunty Ray don't have to carry a knife round with 'er, does she? But I keep ma mouth shut.

He's only gorra single bed. I sez, "Liam, where am I gonna sleep? Shall I jump on the sofa?" He guz, "Don't be daft, it's cold. Gerrin wi' me. It'll be our little secret." An' I'm like, I am gonna sleep in a bed wi' *Liam*? What the fuck is goin' on? He sez, "Yer a rent boy, aren't ya? Don't worry, Ah've done it too." But funnily enough this don't surprise me at all, coz a lotta rent boys are straight or bisexual, or at least they say they are. Clients love that. That's almost as good as havin' a big dick. Or bein' young. Some of 'em only do things wi' men for money, they've got girlfriends an' everythin'! Part of me thinks everyone's a bit gay, deep down. I've just met too many two-faced men. He guz, "D'ya make a lotta money?" So I'm like, "I do alright. D'ya need to borrow some?" Coz I'm thinkin' if I help 'im, he might start treatin' me like a proper mate. But he guz, "Ah've heard ya love to give head." Honestly, the rumours about me!

He guz, "D'ya wanna finish this?" An' hands me the spliff. Then he sez, "Let's go ter bed." I don't really know what to do so I take ma jeans off coz I can't really sleep in them, canna, but it's cold an' I feel a bit stupid so I keep ma T-shirt on. "Cold, innit?" he guz. He's got 'is back to me. "Why don't ya lean into me?" he guz. "Keep warm an' that." I'm like, Oh my God, I can't keep up wi' this. But then I start thinkin', Am I missin' summat here? Like, does he fancy me? Cause I'm terrible at this sorta thing. I'm used to people just comin' up to me an' askin' me if I wanna suck their cock for a tenner. I'm no good at readin' between the lines. Subtle is not ma middle name.

Obviously I'm dead turned on, but what if I've gorrit wrong an' he guz an' tells everyone? Oh God, what if it's a set-up? What if he's just windin' me up to take the piss out of me? He obviously takes a great deal of pleasure in humiliatin' me in front of everyone, it wun't surprise me if they all jumped out an' started laughin' their heads off. I can just see it now, Fag Ash poppin' out from behind the curtain shoutin', "Surprise! As if Liam would fancy *you*! We've gorrit all on camera!" But just as I'm thinkin' it, he reaches back an' feels me. An' it's not to make a fool of me.

TOXIC

He calls me up an' sez he's got summat to tell me, summat he can't say over the phone. Will I come an' meet 'im? I sez, "Sure, I'll come into town. Shall we meet at the Left Lion?" But he sez he can't be seen wi' me coz he don't want anyone findin' out he's gay. Sez, "When ya next goin' cottagin'?" I sez, "Sat'day. Ma GCSEs are comin' up so I do actually have to go to school for a change." He sez, "Where d'ya go, Trinity Square? Or Market Square?" So I tell 'im I were gonna go to the ones by Trent Bridge coz I like the sinks. "Perfect," he guz. "Out the way." Although he sez I'm a 'eadcase coz o' the sink comment.

I love 'em. They're really good quality. Marble, an' that's dead expensive, innit? There were some round the fireplace at the house on Annesley Road, although that were green an' this is black, wi' bits of white runnin' through it. It's cold an' hard an' looks like it's bin here for about a hundred years. It must be Victorian. The wood's started to rot where it meets the edge, but it still looks proper grand to me. Bet the taps would've bin dead shiny back in Olden Times. I like washin' ma hands in these sinks. It feels old fashioned. Sturdy. There's even a bit scooped out the marble for the soap to go – an' they still put actual bars of soap out, although they get this scummy jelly collectin' round 'em. It's probably full of germs, but I like things bein' how they used to be. It could be dead nice, this place, if they did it up. Wish I could've seen these toilets when they were new.

He turns up wearin' a new coat – a denim parker, an' one o' them hats wi' graffiti on it. They sell 'em on the market outside Broadmarsh, but he insists it's the real thing, proper expensive like. It is nice. I want one. He's a hard one to read, Liam. Not like Max. I always felt like Max actually wanted to see me. I never felt like he looked down on me. I don't even know what Liam thinks about me, apart from thinkin' he's better than me. He sez he don't like boys who are girly – OK, so why's he hangin' round wi' me then? It just don't make any sense. The most annoying bit, though, is that the more he makes me feel like dirt, the more I like 'im.

He walks up to the dryer an' pretends to dry 'is hands before he even sez, "Ey up." He looks paranoid. I'm like, "Er, hi Liam", so he guz, "Don't call me that in here." Worram I s'posed to call 'im, Doctor Beat? He could've warned me we were usin' pseudonyms. Not that he'd know a word like that. People do use fake names, but there's only us in here. I ask 'im if he's ever bin here before, but he sez they closed down the ones he used to go in. He's gorra few clients he's bin seein' for years, but no one else knows about it. Sez he's told one of 'em about me. Sez 'is name's Dean.

He's thirty-four. Gay. Pretty normal, apparently, not dead sexy but not mingin' either. Gorra bit of a bald patch an' a belly, but that's nowt compared to what ya see in here. Liam reckons he's got loadsa money. I don't really like the fact that Liam'll get paid for settin' it all up, but it is what it is, innit? He's probably gerrin too old for this client. I bet this Dean'll end up likin' me more. I ask Liam if he's told 'im how old I am, so he guz, "Ah've told 'im ya turnin' sixteen next month, but he's not bothered about that. He wants ya in a bed, not in some shithole like this." Sez, "Can I give 'im yer number?" So I say of course. Well, no sooner am I on the bus home than this Dean starts textin' me. Sez he's heard all about me an' is lookin' forward to meetin' me. Askin' loadsa questions. I run out of credit so he offers to put a fiver on for me. Sez he's dead excited about what he's gonna do to me.

ON THE BEACH

I've not told Lady Die about this Dean. He's made me promise to keep it secret, although I'm dyin' to tell 'er that me an' Liam are now partners in crime. Speakin' of which, I've gorra new wig. Me an' Lady Die nicked it from the Debenhams on Market Square last Thursday. It's not real hair, but it looks proper bo. I felt a bit bad stealin' summat so expensive – it's not like nickin' an eyeliner, is it? – but Die sez it's not our fault we need things other people don't, an' she's gorra point actually. Coz I'd just grow ma own hair if they'd let me. She's already nicked one. It's dead long an' she's always losin' 'er earrings an' findin' 'em in it two weeks later. I'm desperate to give it a wash. They've got these big stairs in Debenhams that no one uses coz everyone just takes the escalator, but I really like 'em. They've got big marble steps an' this wide wooden banister an' I always get déjà vu on 'em. There's like this little room about four floors up wi' loadsa wigs. It's not really connected to the rest of Debenhams. It's not even really on a floor, it's like half-way between the third an' fourth levels. God knows how they make money, coz yer'd never know it were there unless someone showed ya.

It's run by these two old women who sit there smokin' all day. They look like an old pair of leather handbags.

They're quite chilled though, so ya can actually smoke, right there, in the shop. They've bin up there chuffin' away since the sixties, by the sounds of it, coz they've both got dead deep voices. People say, "Ya can always tell if it's a man or a woman by the voice", which might be true a lotta the time, but ma voice is dead feminine so ya can't always go on stereotypes, can ya? I remember when I first called round for Smanfa – I must've bin about nine or ten – 'er mam shouted, "There's a gel wi' a shaved 'ead askin for ya." I mean, for fuck's sake! Smanfa loves that story.

So there ya go, I sound like a girl an' these wig-mongers sound like drag queens, even though they're not. They're easily distracted, so me an' Lady Die were able to get one each. That's terrible, innit? I do actually feel quite guilty about it, but they're so bleddy expensive. Over a hundred pounds! That's a week's wages. The one I got were menna be a hundred an' thirty. For a wig! Lady Die sez that's daylight robbery, so we're only doin' what they're doin' to other people. Sez it serves 'em right. The way she makes it sound, you'd think we were Robin friggin' Hood, stealin' from the rich to give to the poor. I guess we are, in a way.

So these old bags are like, "Are you two in a show?" An' Lady Die starts goin' on about how she's a singer an' I'm thinkin', If she tells 'em she's in an S Club Seven tribute band, I'm gonna scream, so of course the next words out 'er mouth are, "I'm in an S Club Seven tribute band called S Club Heaven." An' I'm thinkin', Don't do it, Die. Whatever you do, do not offer to sing. "D'ya wanna hear me sing? I'm Rachel Stevens." An' I just look at 'er gone out, coz she's Bradley – Rachel's white, for fuck's sake – but they don't know who's who anyway an' just go, "Ah, that's nice, sweetheart. Go on, then." Why does everyone assume I'm in a show? Do I need an excuse to want long hair? Although they probably think yer a pervert or a serial killer if yer not in a show. I just told 'em I'm gay, coz everyone knows gay people love dressin' up. I don't know why Lady Die's so nice to everyone. 'Er an' Fag Ash are always goin' up to strangers like, "Ooh I love yer dress, babe!" an', "Have ya had a good night?" They always find out where the party is though, so I shun't complain really. So as she's singin' away to 'em, I stuff this long red wig in ma bag. Cheers, yer royal highness!

I felt awful when we come out, but this is worram like, innit? I bet they won't even notice till they do a stock check in like four hundred years. Anyway, I bought a wig comb that cost seven pounds, so they have had summat out of me, an' it's not ma fault they don't have better security, is it? No cameras or nowt. They're askin' for it, really. Lady Die's on 'er third wig, the sticky-fingered slag. I'm not doin' it again though, I don't wanna take the piss. An' anyway, I'm not sure I can sit through another performance of "S Club Party" without stranglin' ma best mate. It were worth it, though. Makeup makes ya beautiful, but the hair's the bit that makes ya look like a woman. Lady Die sez, "What would ya rather be – an ugly woman? Or a pretty transsexual?" It's a tough one, but I sez transsexual coz I reckon most guys would rather have sex wi' someone dead pretty, even if they know it's not a real woman.

Wigs keep ya warm in winter while ya waitin' for the bus, which seems to be the thing me an' Lady Die spend most our time doin' these days. But when yer in the club it can get dead hot. I get paranoid sometimes that someone'll pull it off. It only takes one dickhead, an' let's face it, Nottingham's full of 'em. People ask us sometimes, "Is that yer real hair?" An' ya wanna tell 'em to fuck off, but ya have to smile an' say, "No, it's a wig, it's nice, innit?" Or say it's hair extensions, although I don't like lyin'. I wish I could afford extensions, but I cun' anyway coz I can't walk around wi' long hair as a boy. Sometimes people ask us if our boobs are real an' I've come up wi' the perfect response: "Well, yer not imaginin' 'em." I'm always thinkin' of stuff to say back to people.

I pretend I'm stupid when people first meet me. Adults always try an' patronize me coz they think I'm too young to know owt, an' I hate it. I were in the chip shop once, the Food Factory, an' I'd actually bin out as a boy for a change so I had ma black denim jacket from Leicester on when this old faggot come over an' sez, "I bet ya don't know who that is on yer coat, do ya?" I sez, "Che Guevara. An' it's a jacket, not a coat." Obviously I an't gorra fuckin' clue who Che Guevara is, but I made a point of askin' the bloke who sold it me coz ya can't not know who's on the back of ya jacket, can ya? I s'pose I'm gerrin quite grown up now. I'm gonna be sixteen next week. That's positively ancient for a rent boy, innit. I reckon I'm gonna stop smokin'. I just know that as soon as I'm allowed all the fun'll go out of it.

THE LAUNCH

Liam's set up a meetin' wi' this Dean twice now – an' he pulled out at the last minute, both times. Liam sez he's a businessman an' that's just the way it is. But then Dean text me an' asked me if I'd meet 'im without Liam, but I can't coz Liam'd go mad. My nerves are bad enough without keepin' secrets from Liam. He knows some really bad people, I'll never be safe in Notts if I cross 'im. I reckon Dean's tryna get out of payin' 'im, an' just pay me directly. Obviously, I'd prefer that – I don't like the thought of Liam makin' money out me havin' sex – but I can't risk it. He's only just started bein' nice to me. So we're meetin' Dean today now, an' he's promised Liam he won't let us down this time. I can't help thinkin' it's a coincidence that it was ma birthday three days ago, but maybe I'm just over-thinkin' it. Some of 'em actually prefer ya to be underage. It's hard to tell what guz through these men's minds. It's not like I've gorra deep emotional connection with any of 'em, is it?

I am excited, though. Liam sez Dean'll gimme fifty quid an' he mainly just wants to see us playin' with each other. An' he's not bothered that I'm feminine. Liam sez he'll like the fact I shave ma legs an' that. An' if he likes me, which Liam sez he will, he'll probably gimme an extra tenner. I've just gorra funny feelin' that this is gonna be a good 'un, despite all the faffin' about.

But I can tell summat's up as soon as I walk through the door. Liam has the big light on an' is sittin' on the end o' the bed with 'is coat on. I'm like, "Are ya goin' out?" But he sez, "Nah, Ah just wanna be ready." Ready for what, Liam? "Sit down," he guz. It's the only time I've bin here an' he's not bin blarin' out Ja Rule, so I perch on the corner of 'is mattress an' I'm thinkin', I hope this Dean's not let us down again. But then he guz, "Ah've gorran idea." I'm like, "OK." "Well," he sez, "this Dean always brings all 'is bank cards with 'im, coz I've seen 'is wallet." An' I'm like, "Right." Then he looks at me wi' this cheeky glint in 'is eye an' sez, "Why don't we rob 'im?" I'm like, "*Rob 'im?*" "Yeah," he guz. '*Rob 'im.*' I sez, "I'm not robbin' anyone, Liam. Who'd be scared of me?" I don't like sayin' no to 'im, but he'd have bin better off askin' an old friggin' woman. "No," he guz. "Ya don't have to scare 'im. Ah'll get 'is bank cards an' hold 'im here while yo' go ter cash point." I'm like, "How ya gonna get 'is cards off 'im?" So he pulls 'is jacket back an' nods towards 'is armpit. I'm not sure worram lookin' at, at first, but then he pulls it out – an' fuck me, he's gorra gun.

I've never seen a gun before. I din't even really think they had 'em in this country, although ya hear about it on the telly an' that. They don't call it Shottingham for nowt, do they? It's menna be the gun capital o' the UK, after London. Well, that's summat we can all be proud of, innit? I just din't think I knew anybody who'd have one. Even Gaz'd be shocked at this, an' he reckons he's seen everythin' workin' on the doors. Liam asks me if I wanna touch it, an' hands it over. Somehow it's both heavier an' lighter than I thought a gun would be. An' I'm not gonna lie, it's quite excitin'. But for some reason, I just suddenly feel incredibly sad, an' I start thinkin' about the day I made Max come an' see Andy Warhol wi' me. There were an exhibition at Nottingham Castle. I sez, "It's not often ya get summat like that round here, Max. He's proper famous, he 'is." An' they had 'is paintin's, here, in Nottingham. All them soup cans an' that. They even had Marilyn Monroe.

When we come out, I went to the edge o' the castle an' looked down the cliff edge. I'm not very good at workin' out heights, but let's just say it worra long way down. They've built these posh houses into the cliffs, but they just look like doll's houses from up there. A bit further along there's a cave that Uncle Roger used to live in durin' one of 'is "episodes". I climbed onto the wall an' stood up. Max tried to grab me, but I told 'im to let go or I'd jump. Said I'd be alright if he just left me alone. I were terrified, but it felt great. I don't know what it is about heights. I'm scared of 'em. Dead scared. But I'm not scared of fallin'. I'm scared of jumpin'. Coz whenever I'm high up, I get this overwhelmin' urge to just . . . leap off. I'm not suicidal. I don't wanna die or owt. It's just knowin' that ya can. How easy it'd be to do it. An' how summat so simple – so instant – can have the power to change yer life for ever. An' sittin' on the edge of Liam's bed, lookin' at that gun, I feel exactly the same way as I did on the edge o' that cliff. "Alright then, Liam," I go. "Let's do it."

I felt bad. But not that bad. He is, after all, a dirty fuckin' perv. An' to be honest I were buzzin' walkin' down that street knowin' I'd got 'is bank cards in ma back pocket. Liam din't have to hurt 'im or owt. He just showed 'im the gun. He told me it's an imitation, so I were like, "Story of ma life, Liam." Lady Die always sez fake it till ya make it. Fag Ash sez fake it till yer fake as fuck, an' she should know. They look exactly the same on the outside. It's summat to do wi' the mechanism. He wun't tell me where it's from, but I bet it's the Woodies, although it could've bin anyone really, coz Liam knows loadsa dodgy people. I guess I do now. I might even be one. I like misbehavin', I know that. I don't know why though. I just love it. I ran away from home when I were ten, an' I just remember feelin' so happy walkin' down the lane to the dump. When I come back, *News at Ten* were on. Mam were furious.

I got in a car once wi' some old bloke I used to meet in the bogs on 'ucknall market. He looked like the Farmer in ma copy o' *The Three Little Pigs*, so that's what I called 'im. He always had muddy boots on an' a bottle of Listerine in 'is glove compartment, that he made me swig after he'd come in ma mouth coz he sez it stops ya gerrin sexually transmitted diseases. I'm not convinced it does, but it's can't hurt, I s'pose. He said he were takin' me to Dead Man's Wood, but we drove for miles down these long country lanes, then up this massive hill an' back down again. It were like one o' them roads ya see in Canada or summat. An' the further out we went, the more I were thinkin', Worram I gerrin mysen into? There were hardly anyone around, an' I started worryin' that he might murder me, but I kind of liked the excitement. Then he pulled into this car park in the middle o' the woods, full of cars. Sez, "Right, out ya get."

I step out an' the Farmer sez, "Go down that path." I'm feelin' around in ma pockets for a piece of bread or summat, thinkin', I'll leave a trail like Hansel an' Gretel. Although that went wrong, din't it? But it's irrelevant anyway, coz I an't got any fuckin' bread, have I, coz it's not Olden Times an' who the fuck keeps bread in their pockets. We go deeper into these woods an' the sun's beginnin' to go down. As we get further in, I start to notice rubbish. A used condom. Pages from a porno. Empty beer cans. Then I see two men up ahead, one suckin' the other one off. The Farmer guz, "Why don't ya go up to 'em? They'll be pleased to see ya."

They were. The one who's stood up looks at me an' went, "D'ya wanna go, lad?" Then he turns to the Farmer, like he's lookin' for permission. The Farmer went, "Go on, have a go on 'im." But he were talkin' to the man, not me. Like he owned me. But I liked it. I liked it a lot. By the end, there must've bin about fifteen of 'em. It were dark by then, but they must have known how young I was. I've got no meat on me as it is, an' this were two years ago. I were centre of attention. They were all fightin' to be wi' me. They pulled ma legs apart an' I could feel all these hands, touchin' me all over. None of 'em were rough or owt. It were gentle. The thing that sticks wi' me the most though is that no one said a word. Like it weren't real if we din't say it out loud. An' then one of 'em got inside me. I din't even see 'is face. So I've bin fucked by someone an' I wun't know 'im from Adam if he tapped me on the shoulder right now an' asked for a light. It's bad, innit? But the worst thing is, I loved it.

Just like I loved seein' that money come out that cash-point. There's summat wrong wi' me, I know there is. I'm a problem child. But at least I'm not a hypocrite. At least I'm not married. At least I know I'm bad. Dean has a limit on how much he can withdraw in one day, so I could only get two hundred pounds on each card. After midnight, I could try again. I got there at ten to. Liam had timed it on purpose. Clever, innee? There were three cards. One thousand two hundred pounds. I mean, I knew it was wrong. An' yeah, I thought about callin' the police or summat, but how could I? I'd be dead meat if I snitched on Liam. He din't count the money till he'd let Dean go, which made me feel better coz I cun' look 'im in the eye. I thought Liam were gonna fuck me over, but he gave me seven hundred pounds. That's a lot, innit? Money don't grow on trees, ya know.

LADY (HEAR ME TONIGHT)

Peter sez ya don't have to say "hot" if ya say "boilin'", coz all boilin' water is hot "by definition". But that's how I've always said it – I pulled a pan of boilin' hot water on me when I worra baby. He sez I can't have bin a baby either, I worra toddler if I could stand up. He's so clever, innee? He's teachin' me how to speak properly. He sez I'm like Eliza Doolittle. Fuck knows what that is, but he seems to find it amusin'. Mam sez she only took 'er eyes off me for a split second. Someone were boilin' eggs an' the handle were hangin' off the edge o' the cooker – I reached up an' grabbed it. I'd only just learned how to walk. Went all over ma chest. Mam sez I were lucky it din't go on ma face. I could've bin like one o' them people ya see on telly.

Mam had to run upstairs wi' me an' put me under the shower wi' cold water. She sez ma skin were hangin' off like tissue paper. It were at Aunty Ray's, back when Mammar Joe still lived there. They've gorran "avocado" green bathtub an' see-through taps that say Armitage Shanks on 'em. There's always a half-used bar of Imperial Leather on the sink. I love that one coz it's gorra little foil label on it. Gaz uses Pears. Mam gets Dove. I cun' tell ya what an avocado were if ma life depended on it, but whatever it is, that's the colour o' that bath. It's bin like it since before I were born, so I can really picture the scene: Mam, hangin' over it, screamin', ma skin droppin' off in little shreds, white on avocado. She sez the ambulance took ages.

They could only afford to live in that house coz Old Mother 'ubbard won the pools in the seventies. Nottingham Forest came round with a great big cheque an' Mammar Joe had to pretend to open the door an' act surprised while they took pictures. They did a story about it in the *Nottingham Post*. Aunty Ray's gorrit, she cut it out an' put it in 'er photo album. They won ten-thousand grand! That's a lot, innit? That's how they could afford an avocado bath. Mam sez they're dead expensive.

They put all the kids that have bin burned on the same ward an' Mam sez the boy next to me were in a right old state. 'Is mam had started runnin' 'im a bath by fillin' it up wi' just the hot tap. Well, it must have bin really hot coz he jumped in an' got burned all the way up to 'is neck. 'Is whole body! It's true what they say, there's always someone worse off. That's why you've gorra be grateful for what you've got. All I remember is havin' to wear a vest an' Mammar Joe puttin' special cream on it, coz afterwards she'd say, "Right, let's see if Old Mother 'ubbard's got owt hidin' at the back o' the cupboard" an' then pull out some Nesquik. Yer menna add milk, but I like it straight out the packet with a teaspoon. Mammar Joe still makes me put Nivea on ma chest before bed. She swears by it. She puts it on 'er face an' I do too now coz she still looks dead young for a mammar. She's gonna be fifty next. Ma chest's a lot better these days. When I were little it looked like Freddy Krueger but it's not as bad now coz it's stretched as I've grown. I've gorra funny nipple, though. It looks like cheese on toast.

They had to take some skin from ma thigh an' make a graft from it. I've never really bin ashamed of it or owt when we've gone swimmin'. I'm too busy worryin' about ma general mannerisms, to be honest. Gaz hit me so hard one time that he bruised the bottom of ma back an' Mammar Joe sez I cun' go swimmin' that week coz I might get taken into care. I love swimmin'. I like takin' a deep breath an' goin' all the way to the bottom. I wonder sometimes what ma chest would look like if they cloned me. It's weird when I try an' think about not havin' it, coz it's just always bin there. It'd be good if I could clone mysen though, eh? I'm not really bothered about ma scar, but there's loads of other stuff I'd make different. For starters, I'd be a girl. Obviously. I've always felt like a girl. But they won't let me.

I cun' relax in Lovezoo. They had the smoke machine on, an' I kept thinkin' Liam were gonna jump out an' grab me from the shadows. It were like bein' on the friggin' ghost train at Goose Fair. No one were out though, apart from Die, obviously. She sez no one ever has any money after New Year's. So of course I happened to look fuckin' amazin'. Me an' Fag Ash ended up havin' this massive fall-out coz she stole ma man off me – literally the only fit guy in there – who'd bin chattin' me up all night. I sez, "Erm, 'scuse me lay-deh, but I think you'll find he were talkin' to me first", but she were like, "Actually I saw 'im arrive, so get fucked." I were fumin'. Why does she do it? I'm sick of 'er. Well, it don't matter now coz I won't be goin' out with any of 'em, ever again. An' I'm never takin' drugs again either.

It started wi' speed. The guy had dropped some in ma drink before Fag Ash spoiled ma fun, so me an' Lady Die were buzzin' come midnight. Just dropped it in at the bar, blatantly. I don't even like speed. It's alright if ya wanna stay awake for three days an' clean yer room, but I'm terrible on no sleep. It just makes me anxious. But then we both get proper mashed up, so I'm like, I don't even give a fuck. I sez, "He's all yours, Pavash. Knock yersen out. Before I do, ya rancid bitch." I hope she gets

SARS. I don't stay mad for long though coz soon enough Sticky Nikki turns up an' starts givin' us bumps, an' *then* I find a pill on the toilet floor. A Superman. Die were like, "Yo're tekkin' the fuckin' piss" – then halves it wi' me. Waste not, want not, eh? I hate losin' drugs coz ya just know some miserable fucker'll end up flushin' 'em down the loo or summat. Well, the good people of Lovezoo wun't, but not everywhere's Lovezoo, sadly. I reckon if ya find drugs that some honest, God-fearin' fuckhead has left behind in the confusion o' their mind-altered night out, ya owe it to party people the world over to ingest that shit on their behalf. So we did.

As ya can imagine, me an' the People's Princess are pretty fuckin' battered by this point. We leave Lovezoo coz I can't be doin' wi' Mr Speed an' that poisonous witch killin' ma vibe for a minute longer. As we're walkin' up to Market Square, this car full of Asian guys shouts us over. Lady Die does 'er bimbo routine – "Hiya, darlin'" – an' asks 'em for a light, so we stand there havin' a fag. An' I'm sayin' nowt, knowin' it'll make 'em even more intrigued wi' me. They're goin' down Leicester. Do we wanna join 'em. I ask Die if we can have a quick girl chat coz I reckon it could be dangerous if they find out our little secret. She sez it'll be fine though coz we're not pretendin' to be girls, we're just us, an' it's none o' their business anyway. She's eighteen, so technically ma responsible adult. "He's offerin' us a lift," she guz. "Not a hand in marriage. We don't owe 'em nuffin." I'm not entirely sure they'd see it that way, but we both look good, so I'm like, whatever. Fuck it.

We end up ditchin' 'em at the first bar anyway – "See ya later, guys, thanks for the lift!" So we try that twenty-four-hour place an' who do we bump into but Leicester Mike, or, as Lady Die calls 'im, Go-Go Gadget Dick, coz apparently it just keeps growin' an' growin'. I mean, I'm not one for sloppy seconds usually, but I wun't say no to 'im. He's a chemistry teacher. Twenty-seven. Dead fit. Always has loadsa pills on 'im – an' tonight's no exception. He guz, "Well I never, Nottingham's leading shoplifters!" Twelve pills later an' ma wig's fallin' off on the dancefloor an' I don't even care. The bouncers come over an' congratulate us on bein' "the best female imper-sonators" they've ever seen. No one else seems to have noticed, thank God, coz they're all battered, but I'm paranoid they're gonna start tellin' people. I s'pose it's better than the time we cun' get into a bar coz the man-ager said they had a no drag queen policy. Lady Die sez, "We're princesses, not queens", but I din't even wanna go in after that. Coz I don't feel like I'm "dressin' up" when I go out. I just feel like me.

An' I honestly don't think I've ever looked more beau-tiful. Lady Die sez I look like Madonna in the "Nothin' Really Matters" video – big wide eyes, bright red lips an' long straight hair. I reckon she looks like the black 'un from Sugababes tonight, so she's dead happy wi' that. This fit guy comes on to us an' we end up takin' 'im to the toilets. It's not even a gay club. We're gonna end up murdered one o' these days. He were cool when we told 'im though – he wanted us to fuck 'im, but I'd never do that. I'm the girl. I want the man to do it to me. Die were

like, "Nah, man. Not here. That's rank. I'm a Christian."
But we were pretty wasted so I shoved the toilet brush
handle up 'im while Lady Die wanked 'im off, an' he
ended up comin' all over the toilet seat like a Roman
friggin' candle. We had to ask the next cubicle to pass
some bog roll under.

Well anyway, he giz us some GBH, an' oh, that's it
then. I end up proper hallucinatin'. I din't actually think
it were possible to sleep through full-blast hard house,
but ya learn summat new every day, don't ya? I open ma
eyes an' there's these Manga mousses wavin' at me from
the dancefloor. I'm like, "Die, I'm seein' cartoons. I don't
think I've ever bin so out of control in public before –
innit marvellous?" An' it is. But the absolutely best part,
the big fat juicy fuckin' cherry on the cake, is knowin'
that Fag Ash'll be *so* jealous when she finds out, which
she will, as soon as I see 'er, coz I'm gonna tell 'er about
it in all its glorious detail.

But what guz up must come down. Now listen, I've
done some walks of shame. But there's rough an' there's
rough, d'ya know worra mean? An' as we head into the
daylight, I catch a glimpse of Lady Die, an' oh God, it's
like two different people. She sez, "What ya starin' at me
like that for?" So I'm like, "I'm not bein' funny, babe,
but ya look like an absolute bastard." She sez, "Ya should
look in a mirror sometime", but mine's dirty so I try
someone's rear-view mirror. It's bad. I barely look like a
human bein', let alone a girl. Ma makeup's rottin' off,
there's lines where I've bin sweatin', an' ma eyes are all
smudged. I try an' tidy 'em up a bit, but Lady Die's goin',

"Oi, come here. Get away", an' right as I'm thinkin', What is 'er friggin' problem? I look through the window an' there's a family of four sat inside, starin' at me in horror. I go, "Oh sorry. I din't see ya", go to get up, then fall over. It's two in the afternoon. It's a wonder I've not bin locked up by now.

When I catch up wi' Lady Die I sez, "I can't be doin' wi' this", but she's just like, "Just act normal." But we're not normal, are we? Not by a very long stretch o' the imagination, an' that's at the best of times. I just wanna get away from the club before people start comin' out. I don't want everyone who thought we were beautiful seein' us in the daylight. It's a real Cinderella moment, this. I'm like, "Come on, let's go to a toilet an' sort oursens out." So we go to the shoppin' centre an' wash our faces in the ladies loos. God knows what we must've looked like, but there's no way I'm gerrin a train back to Nottingham without sortin' mysen out. We do look a lot better for it after though, so we go an' nick summat warm to wear from Jane Norman – or as I like to call it, *Jane Normal*, coz the clothes are dead borin'. We must be the least inconspicuous shoplifters in Britain, but I reckon we get away with it coz shop assistants are too busy tryna work out if we're trannies. Serves 'em right, if ya ask me. I hope it gets taken off their wages. I gorra turquoise jacket that shows off ma belly an' Die gorra a black cardigan. She's very classy sometimes, Die. Almost ladylike.

Now we're in the smoking carriage, pretendin' to sleep. We actually did have enough money to get tickets, or at least I did, but we've skanked it anyway. Why pay? We just pretend to be conked out when the ticket man comes coz Die sez they're not allowed to touch ya. We can't look that bad though coz the guy sat opposite stuck up for us when the ticket man started shoutin', an' he wun't have come to our defence if he thought we were transsexuals, would he? But now he's gerrin off at Loughborough. I wanna say thank you. Ya know, show 'im how grateful we are, but I don't wanna risk the inspector comin' back, so I just whisper, "Farewell, ma hero."

SINCERE

Comedown don't even cover it. We go to Peter's coz we're runnin' low on fags – not to mention money – but we can't sleep, so we call Fag Ash. She's wi' Liam an' Nikki, an' all them lot. They've not bin to sleep either. Fag Ash guz, "The only way to stop a comedown is to come back up again", an' I can't argue wi' that so we tell 'em we'll get Peter to drop us off in a bit. I don't really wanna see Liam, but I can't go home like this, canna? Peter sez we look like we need droppin' in a cattle dip, an' makes us jump in the shower before we can sit on 'is new settee. He's goin', "Are you sure you want to go back out? Don't make yourselves ill." An' I'm thinkin', I'd have gone back to Mammar Joe's if I wanted all this. I go, "Peter, I know yer as old as ma mammar, but d'ya have to sound like 'er?" an' instantly regret it. He's only bein' nice. "Fine," he sez. "Thou can do what thou likes", which means he's pissed off. Me an' Die start gerrin ready. I don't know why we are the way we are, but we are.

Them lot are all round Adam's, Fag Ash's mate. He's a makeup artist. He works at Mac an' has all 'is stuff with 'im, so I ask 'im if he'll sort me out an' he sez, "Yeah, of course, I'd love to have a go on that face", which Fag Ash don't like one little bit. While he's doin' it I start tellin' everyone about what a great time me an' Lady Die

121

have had in Leicester, although I din't say owt about the thing wi' the toilet brush. I exaggerate a few bits, too, to make it sound even better an' annoy Fag Ash, which it does. She always takes the bait, that one. She's like a fuckin' carp. I go, "Ah, it's a shame ya din't come, babe. But ya looked like ya were havin' so much fun wi' that guy when we left." Although I shun't have set 'er off really coz then she starts bein' dead passive-aggressive an' there's this awkward atmosphere, so Adam sez, "Right, let's go out." NG1's dead again. Adam's made me look like summat out of a sci-fi movie, wi' silver eye-shadow an' ma contact lenses. I went out as a boy on Friday, a girl last night, an' androgynous tonight. It just feels appropriate, coz I don't feel like a boy or a girl tonight. I feel like a cyborg, an' I look like one.

We do some more speed, an' it's not that bad actually. Lady Die perks up – like a phoenix, risen from the ashtrays – an' starts shockin' out to Lisa Maffia. I would say, "God knows where she gets 'er energy", but it comes in little white lines off the back o' toilet seats. Dirty D an' everyone else turns up an' Fag Ash is still wearin' the dress she had on on Friday, although she swears blind she's bin home an' had a bath. To be fair, if I had a dress like that I wun't take it off all weekend either. She does ma 'ead in, but I do love 'er. She is funny. But then Lady Die sez she's goin' home coz she's had enough. I sez, "*Goin' home? Had enough?*" I've never known 'er to have had "enough" all the time we've bin mates, an' she an't bin home since 1999. But I'm buzzin', coz I've actually outlasted Lady Die for once. Everyone's tellin' me I'm proper hardcore now. Fag Ash sez, "Let's go back to mine." They're playin' "Outta Space" an' I'm feelin' good, but then Liam grabs me by the arm as I'm goin' to the cloakroom an' sez, "Ya better not have said owt to anyone", so I go, "No, of course not, Liam."

The moment we get to Asha's he starts windin' me up though, makin' me paranoid an' that. There's always someone like that at parties, tryna mess wi' yer 'ead. Truth be told, it's usually me. But I don't do it the way Liam does. He takes it too far, till the other person's genuinely freakin' out. Like I am now. The rest of 'em go upstairs an' I'm just laid on the floor in the livin' room an' can't move. Liam's the only one who stays behind wi' me, an' he's goin', "D'ya hear that?" an' I'm like, "Hear what?" an' he's like, "Oh, it's probably nuffin'", an' all that crap. Yeah, yeah, Liam. I know what yer doin'. But even though I know he's doin' it on purpose, it's still gerrin to me.

They come back down eventually. I reckon they've bin doin' more coke an' din't wanna share it with us, which is a bit rude but I'm not even bothered coz I'm already wasted an' Liam's bin feedin' me bumps of K. But where are ma fags? I've bin practically chain-smokin' all night burra can't remember when I last had 'em. I look in ma bag, under the chair, everywhere. I'm freakin' out. Then Liam pulls 'em out the back o' the sofa an' sez, "Lookin' for these, ya dickhead?" wi' this cruel grin on 'is face. I try an' snatch 'em off 'im, but he makes me beg an' I'm too tired to argue with 'im, so I do, I beg.

Like a dog. I spark up, take a drag, an' I'm thinkin', Why does he wanna make me look stupid? Is he jealous? Or does he just really hate me? But it tastes funny. I hold it up to gerra closer look, but then I feel this rush of energy, an' ma eyes roll back into ma 'ead. I din't understand what were happenin' at the time, but I realize now that that were the turnin' point.

WHERE'S YOUR HEAD AT

We leave Asha's an' head towards Sneinton Market. I'm tryin' not to walk too close to 'em without makin' it dead obvious. Everythin' they say seems scripted, like someone's feedin' 'em the lines. But who? A white van's comin' up behind us an' I click: they've brought me here to have me kidnapped. Someone's gonna jump out an' grab me an' take me to Russia to work as a sex slave. The modern-day slave trade. I'll never see ma family again. An' all for the price of a packet of fags, no doubt. The van don't stop. It were Nikki's idea to leave the house. She were like, "I know, let's go up ter the windmill." All innocent, likes. Fag Ash guz, "Shall I wear ma pyjamas? Every other Paki round here does." I've never heard 'er talk like that before. She tells everyone she's Egyptian Catholic. It's four o'clock on Monday mornin'. Where are they takin' me? Where the fuckin' fuck are they takin' me? That's what I wanna know. Fag Ash guz, "Why ya so quiet? Cat got yer tongue?" So I'm like, "Ya know what they say, babe, if you've got nowt nice to say."

I'm usually up for stuff like this, but there's just summat dead strange about how they're talkin', like they're all in it together, plottin' against me. I'm gaggin' for a fag, but how can I when I don't know what they've done to 'em? They've done summat to 'em, I know they have.

They don't smell right. I just don't trust 'em. Liam's the worst. He keeps offerin' me more K but I've had enough. They can tell there's summat up wi' me. I'm sixteen years old an' a shy girl for the first time in ma life. Lady Battenberg, where's yer 'ead at? Trapped, Liam, in the incomprehensible maze. An' you've fuckin' put me here, ya 'orrible bastard. I run away.

They're callin' after me, but I just run an' run. Ma legs are killin' me, but I'd rather be killed by ma legs than than fall prey to their dastardly schemes. Schemin', schemin' witches, the lot of 'em! I don't care what they think, I've gorra get as far away as fast as possible. I reach the top o' the hill an' the windmill's hangin' over me, creakin' with age an' God knows how many ghosts. Where's yer 'ead at? I'm in a dark, dark town, Liam, on a dark, dark street. *Ich würde lieber in der stadt wohnen.* Learned that in German. An' a little voice inside ma 'ead's tellin' me, you've gorra go to the city! Coz where am I, really? Like, really? Rottingham? Or Rome? I'm not even sure this is England, any more.

The sky's purple an' the moon is yellow an' fat, pokin' out from behind clouds of cotton wool like a picture in a children's book. The wind's whisperin' through the trees an' we're in Victorian times, but we can't be really, can we? Coz the houses wun't look old an' there wun't be cars parked everywhere. Makes ya think though, don't it? I keep to the middle o' the road in case someone jumps out at me. Better to be safe than sorry. I look back an' the coven of divas are chasin' me, like zombies, vampires, callin' me, but I'm too far away now. They'll never catch me. When I look, they've gone. When I look again, they're tiny ants. I could reach out an' touch 'em.

When I were little, Aunty Ray had a book where these kids are tryna get to this fabulous city, but no matter how far they go, they don't get any further. They walk for miles an' miles, but the city never gets any closer an' they keep passin' the same bush. I can't remember how it ended. I don't think we finished the book. I wish we had, I wish I knew where to go. Is that another white van? I thought I'd be safe in the centre, but now I'm here I'm not so sure. Wait. What if it's the same one? Oh God. It is. It has to be. No way is that a coincidence. There's no such thing as coincidences. I don't know what to do. I've gorra be safe here. It's Nottingham. They don't control everythin'! Do they? No, that's bananas! Just stay where the cameras can see ya. Peter sez there's cameras everywhere, these days.

I talk better when I'm off ma 'ead.

I can't go inside the taxi rank. But I can't just stand in the middle of Parliament Street, I look like Edward Scissorhands. There's no way I'm riskin' a taxi all the way home. They might be in on it. I know, it sounds far-fetched. But it wun't be that hard to plant someone an' by the time I see he's taken a wrong turn, it'll be too late. I could get 'im to take me to the police station though, an' if he don't go straight there, I'll just open the door an' jump out. If he locks 'em, I'll smash the windows. Kick 'em in wi' ma Kickers. It's not ideal, but we don't live in an ideal world, do we? I can't risk that white van comin' back. What choice have I got?

It's dead bright in the police station. The front desk's empty so I press the bell an' a woman appears. What the fuck am I gonna say? "I need to speak to someone. I think ma friends are after me." She looks at me like I'm a freak an' guz to find someone. There's a camera in the corner. Green lino. Blue Monday. Big Brother. We're live on Channel 4, please do not say fuck or bogger. Can't get what it feels like for a girl out of ma 'ead. Now it's the theme tune from *The Bill*. Oh God. I've just thought, What if they knew I'd come here? What if they've planted drugs on me? What if I'm doin' *exactly* what they want me to do? An' I can't help but laugh. Coz you've gorra give it to 'em, really. They're dead clever. But guess who's even cleverer? I run out.

I'll stay here till seven. It's ten past six now an' it's startin' to get light. This bench were the safest place I could think of. Look, there's Fag Ash on the corner, wearin' glitter an' a big pink wig, handin' out flyers on New Year's Eve. "Pink party, pink champagne," she's tellin' 'em. I'd never heard of it before. An' look, there's me across the road, gerrin felt up by that guy who looks like the one wi' the funny eye from So Solid Crew. I din't know anyone were watchin' till the headlights come on. Sandstorm blarin' out. That 'orrible queen who cun' believe ma eyelashes were real. My lashes! My sand-wiches! My rules! I don't care if I sound like Eliza fuckin' Doolittle, Peter.

I used to be scared of Bananaman when I were little. I din't like 'is voice. The boy eats a banana an' turns into 'im, an' I just hated it. Still sends a shiver down ma spine.

All sorts can happen when you eat a banana. No, never look someone in the eye while you're chewin' on one o' them. Everyone knows that. I'll be safe here though. Lookin' back. Over ma shoulder. I've got that song in ma 'ead. Coz I keep lookin' back. Over ma shoulder. When I'm not inspectin' the fags, that is. They've bin dipped in summat. Marks all over 'em. Yellow, gold an' green. Are they the colours from Karma Chameleon? I'm not sure, but it's all connected, innit? I wish I'd bin around in the eighties. Human League's from Leicester. The things that dreams are made of. Twenty-one seconds to go.

Maybe it were poppers. Or GBH. I'll have to go an' get 'em tested in the cold light of day. But tested for what? When enough people start movin' about I'll walk up to Vicky Centre bus station an' catch the 45 to Old Mother 'ubbard's. Brimful of Asha. She's like the old woman who lives in a shoe. Hannah Bailey's dad drives that bus sometimes. I make 'em laugh, I do. Ah do. We laugh our 'eads off, we do. Off our 'eads, we are. Coz sometimes, just sometimes, you've gorra laugh – or else ya cry. But what if it's the same thing?

Why would Mammar Joe try an' poison me? I can't stop thinkin' about it. I went to the doctor's but he don't believe me. Maybe he's in on it too? I know, I know. I'm bein' ridiculous. He sez there's nowt to worry about so I guess I'll just have to wait an' see, won't I? He don't think I've gorra heroin addiction, though. He just looked at me gone out when I sez that, like I were mental or summat. He probably just thinks I'm an attention-seeker. Everyone else does.

Smanfa cried when she saw me. I sez, "Don't start, I'm menna be the attention-seeker – even Doctor Finchley sez so. It's an official diagnosis now." I don't look *that* bad. But she seemed genuinely upset. Fuckin' idiot. She were wi' Nicola coz they hang out all the time now, they're even goin' on holiday together next month. I've not bin invited. So that's nice for 'em, innit? They can go on about how bad drugs are, an' how fuckin' superior they are for not takin' 'em. Smanfa sez I look really ill. No shit Sherlock! Sez I look dead skinny. I don't think it's as bad as what she's makin' out, but it is pretty bad, if I'm honest. I've got spots all over ma face an' ma skin's grey. I've got massive dark circles that makeup only seems to make worse an' ma eyebrow bar fell out last night. I were on the futon at Mammar Joe's watchin'

Who Wants to be a Millionaire? an' I just felt summat drop
into ma soup. The skin's wore so thin it just split open.
I'm literally rottin' away.

Ma lips are cracked no matter how much water I drink
or how much Vaseline I put on 'em. The thing that's
most scared me though is summat Smanfa din't even
see. After she left I looked in the bathroom mirror, an'
the back of ma throat were *black*. Not grey. Not green.
Not brown. Black. I look dead. I thought I were hallucinatin' at first, but I weren't. All this black phlegm an'
bruised tissue. I cun' even show Mammar Joe. She's
dead worried about me too, but I feel quite distant from
'er, actually. I know she's on ma side really, but I've just
not felt right round 'er since the other day. Yeah, I know,
why on earth would Mammar Joe poison me? I know
I'm goin' mad. But I'm just not sure I can trust 'er one
hundred per cent. Smanfa looked at me like I worra 'eadcase when I told 'er that, but ya can never trust anyone
completely, can ya? Look at Harold Shipman.

I know I'm bein' ridiculous. I hope I am, anyway. Coz
Mammar Joe's the only person I've always felt I could
trust. She wun't hurt a fly. Mammar Joe's the sorta person who'd go hungry to let ya have 'er last bit of food.
Me an' Lady Die turned up unannounced once an' she
were like, "Oh dear, it's like Old Mother 'ubbard's round
here", an' gave us 'er last tin o' beans. She's always made
me feel welcome, I could knock on 'er door any hour an'
I know she'd be pleased to see me. But I can't help it.
"Paranoia'll destroy ya," as Fag Ash always sez. I like the
other one though. "Just coz yer bein' paranoid don't

mean they're not out to get ya." Coz it's true! But why would Mammar Joe try an' poison me?

I were watchin' *EastEnders* under the quilt when she brought me Heinz fuckin' soup again. All I've had to eat for the past week is soup an' cheese sandwiches, but it din't taste right. An' it had this colourful film floatin' on it. She were like, "Get that down yer neck. You'll be rate in no time." "Rate" is how Mammar Joe sez "alright". But there were just summat in 'er voice that din't sound right to me, like someone playin' the wrong note in the back of a song. I were thinkin', Why is she sayin' I'll be alright? How does she know? An' what the fuck is tomato' soup gonna do?

I've still got the fags. Malboro. Reds. I'm gonna show 'em Peter an' I'm gonna tell 'im, if I'm imaginin' it, why do they have marks on 'em? Ya can see little splashes. Yellow an' green marks. Mammar Joe can see 'em too. So could Smanfa. Four days later. In the daylight. So it can't all be in ma 'ead, can it? They did summat to these cigarettes, I know they did. I have to find out what. I feel so weak, though. Fag Ash text me on Tuesday, she guz, "What got into you on Sunday?" I thought, I don't know, Asha, you tell me? But I an't replied. Why would Mammar Joe try an' poison me?

"No call, no text, no nuffin." Rather stupidly, I hadn't predicted this. But I can tell it's gonna be bad. I'm on the edge o' the settee. I've kept ma trainers on. Ma 'ead can't deal wi' this. "Ya treat this 'ouse like a fuckin' hotel." Oh yeah, Gaz, you'd make a brilliant hotel manager, you. Guests'd be queuein' up for miles! Imagine the welcome: "Good afternoon, Madame. Can I interest ya in a glass of wine an' a clip round the earhole, ya stupid lil' cunt?" I can't be doin' wi' confrontation though, so I tell 'im I've bin badly. "Mammar Joe's bin lookin' after me. I thought me mam woulda told ya.' It's true, I'm not very well. Not very well at all. "Ya could've messaged me," he guz. "Ya could've called Mammar Joe," I go. Only in ma 'ead, though. I feel strange. Detached.

Then he's like, "D'ya think I were born yesterday?" An' I have to bite ma tongue again coz it wun't surprise me at all, actually. I look out the window an' there's a sparrow on the front wall peckin' at the moss between the bricks. It smells like gravestones when it's damp. They took the railin's away durin' the war an' used the iron to make weapons. I sat on it once an' gorra mark on ma jeans that wun't come out no matter how many times I put 'em in the wash, just one of many things on the list of stupid stuff I've done. It were pissin' it down on the way an' the hydrangea's covered wi' rain drops. It's pink. Aunty Ray's is purple. I prefer hers.

"Ya waltz in here an' think ya can do as ya please. Ya prance around like a little fuckin' gel, always gorra be different, always wantin' attention. What sorta fuckin' lad are ya? None of yer cousins are like this." Would that be ma cousin who works in a dodgy factory changing the labels on tinned food so shops can sell 'em past their sell-by date? Or the heroin addict? But I just sit an' enjoy the performance, coz who's the attention-seeker now? Don't let me interrupt yer monologue, Gaz. "All ya care about is yersen – just like ya mother, yo' are!"

When I first got ma mobile, I used to withhold ma number an' call the landline in the middle o' the night. I'd wait till I could hear 'im snorin', then I'd hear 'im goin', "Who the bleedin' hell is callin' at this time o' night?" an' I'd lay there, cramped up wi' laughter. I'd just let it ring an' ring till eventually I'd hear 'im jump out of bed an' bomb downstairs. When I heard the livin' room door fling open – an' that he were just about to reach the phone – I'd hang up. He went absolutely mental. An' the moment he got back into bed, I'd do it again. He disconnected the phone in the end. I'd have done it every night if I could, but I had to be careful in case he ever worked it out. An' as he's stood there, goin' on at me, I start thinkin' about it, an' how angry he got. An' I start laughin'. I can't help it. He guz, "Think it's funny, do ya? Well, ya can fuck off back to wherever you've bin as far as I'm concerned." I look out the window an' see the sparrow fly off.

He guz, "Ya walk out that door a boy. But one day

134

you'll come back, an' when ya do you'll be a man." I mean, I wun't hold your breath, Gaz. But d'ya know what? Leavin's a brilliant idea. Mint. Best you've ever 'ad. Coz I'm sixteen an' I can do worra want now. D'ya even know how old I am? Coz I seemed to miss ma birthday card from ya this year. Mammar Rita must've forgotten, but then ya do have so many children for 'er to keep track o' these days, don't ya? I don't know if it's even occurred to ya that I'm old enough to leave, but you've said it now, an' I don't need askin' twice. I don't say any o' this out loud, mind. In fact, I don't intend on sayin' another word to dear old Pappa for the rest of ma life. This little bird's fallen out o' that nest now.

SHE WANTS TO MOVE

I called Peter earlier an told 'im everythin'. He sez I'm ma own worst enemy. Sez it sounds like a psychosis. Well, whatever it was, it weren't good. I can't believe I thought Mammar Joe were tryna poison me. I must be really losin' the plot if I think Old Mother 'ubbard's against me – the only thing she's guilty of is havin' bare friggin' cupboards. All she's ever done is love an' look after me. 'Er an' Aunty Ray are the only ones who've always bin there for me. I feel so bad for thinkin' it now. Everyone thought Mammar Joe were me mam when I were little, coz she used to take me everywhere. She's more like me mam than me mam. It's nice havin' a young Mammar coz it means she'll be around for ages. Me mam too. We can all get old together.

I don't really have any grandads. Gaz don't speak to 'is dad. He were the same as Gaz by the sounds of it, worse actually. Gaz took me to see 'im once, but that's the only time I've met 'im. Me mam's dad left Mammar Joe when she were pregnant. We don't know owt about 'im. Mammar Joe won't talk about it. Mam always sez Mammar Joe don't know who he is. She asked 'er once, she went, "Ya can tell me, ya know, if ya went to a party or summat – *it was the sixties*." Which made me laugh coz

I'm pretty sure Mammar Joe wun't do owt like that. She seemed dead upset, so Mam dropped it.

But it makes ya wonder, don't it? They did all sorts back then, by the sounds of it. Mammar Joe sez that if it had bin the earlier sixties they might have tried to take Mam away from 'er, coz she worra single mam an' that. That's what they did back then, they sent 'em to be adopted. Mam sez people used to look down their nose at 'er in the eighties, coz she worra teenage single mum too, but they din't take people's babies away by then. In fact, they gave 'er a council house.

I love Mammar Joe, but I can't stay here. I can't even go to the shop for a pint of milk. There's always a gang of lads hangin' round near the shop, right outside the door-way. If I try an' go in, one of 'em'll stick out a leg or summat an' trip me up. Or shout, "Oi, Byron, ya bender, what ya gerrin from the shop? A carrot to stick up yer arse?" Well, I'm not Byron the Bender when I'm in Nottingham. An' there are people who actually respect me an' think I'm good. So why would I wanna stay round here?

D'ya know how I know I love Max? Like, really, really love 'im? Coz if he asked me to go to Spain with 'im tomorrow, I'd go. I'd still go. I'd just fly out there, like that. An' I don't even wanna live abroad, I love it here. It's called Great Britain for a reason. I don't get why people are always sayin' how much they hate this coun-try. In other countries, ya have wars an' freak weather an' there's no NHS. But it don't matter coz he's not askin' me to move, is he? I cried mysen to sleep last night, thinkin' about what we had. It were like every-thin' were alright when I were with 'im. I just felt like, I dunno, like nowt could hurt me. Like I weren't bothered about owt. I thought about Gaz an' all them twats at school, an' I just hate 'em. They an't gorra clue how I feel or what's inside me. They don't know how much love I've got. Max is the only person who understood me, an' now I've lost 'im.

I've always felt like I've had this light inside of me, that other people are tryna put out. I know it sounds corny, but I don't know how else to explain it. But the thing is, it's ma job to protect this light. So I can't let 'em win. I can't let 'em extinguish it. But more than that, I can't ruin things for mysen. Peter sez I'm ma own worst enemy an' I hate 'im for always bein' right, but he is. An' I am. I've brought most ma problems on mysen, if I'm honest, but I don't know how to stop. Which makes me so mad, coz I know there's summat better for me out there, that I were meant for more than this. I come home with a bad report from school once an' Gaz were so angry, he kept goin', "Ya could piss this if ya wanted. An' yer wastin' yer brains. I want ya to have a better life than I've had son."

Well I wanna better life too. I don't know worram gonna do, or how I'm gonna do it, but I'm gonna do summat dead good, I just know I am. Coz I've got the ability, an' not everyone has that. So I'm makin' a prom-ise to mysen now, to succeed, no matter what. I'm gonna prevail. Peter told me that word. It means to win, to prosper, to succeed. An' that's worrav gorra do – prevail. I must prevail.

CALL ON ME

I've gorra job in a call centre now. Sticky Nikki works there an' sez they had a work party the other week an' put five hundred pounds behind the bar coz they'd had a good month. Apparently there's a woman who works there who can get ya any drugs ya want, although I'm havin' a break from all that. But how cool is that? It's called Robin Hood Resorts. Ya take a page out the phone book an' call people up an' get 'em to go to this meetin' where they try an' sell 'em timeshare. Ya get a script, it guz, 'Hello, is that Mr or Mrs Whatsyerface? I'm callin' from Robin Hood Resorts. Can I confirm your address is –" An' then ya read it out the phonebook.

It's called cold-callin'. If they ask ya where ya got the number, ya have to say, "Either you or your partner filled in one of our marketin' questionnaires in the past two years. Can I ask, have you bin abroad within that timeframe? As that's the most likely place you provided us with your details." That's a trick to find out if they can afford holidays. I'm quite good at sounding posh. Ya have to ask 'em if they're a homeowner with a household income in excess of forty thousand pounds. Coz if they do that means they're loaded. It's so manipulative. What worries me though is that I'm dead good at it, coz I can talk for England, me. I've only bin there a week an' I've already set up six meetin's.

Some people get really mad wi' ya an' threaten to call the police, but you'd be amazed how many fall for it. It turns out it's not just 'ucknall – there's stupid people all over the country. I've bin callin' an area called Kidderminster. I'd never heard of it before but they've gorra dead weird accent, it's even worse than Notts. I don't like lyin' to people though, so I'm always just honest with 'em, even though yer not s'posed to. The meetin's last about two hours an' I think they do pressure 'em a bit, but the thing is, if they like travellin', it is a good deal. Or at least that's what the manager sez. But it's gorra be legal, eh? There's about forty of us in the office, we can't all be breakin' the law – can we? I actually feel more guilty about this than havin' sex for money. At least that's honest.

If I really click wi' someone I just tell 'em straight up that I get a commission if they turn up, an' I could really do wi' the money. It's true. An' people like honesty. It hurts when people shout or hang up, but our team leader Stella sez, "Every no brings ya closer to a yes. Even if only one person in a hundred sez yes, all you've gorra do is keep goin'." Worst case, you ask ninety-nine people, an' they say no. But what does it matter? Coz when ya get that yes, it's all worth it. We get paid our bonus whether or not they buy the timeshare. I get ten pounds for every couple that turns up. If ya get ten couples to attend in one week, ya get the biggest bonus the company offers – two hundred pounds. Only one person has achieved that so far so she's allowed to smoke in the office. The rest of us have to go outside, even when it's cold.

I've told Mammar Joe I'm leavin' to be closer to work now school's done. She asked me if I'm a prostitute. I cun' believe it. I sez, "What makes ya say that?" She sez I'm always leavin' late, in short skirts, an' not comin' back till God knows when. An' where do I get all ma money. She knows I've got cash coz I tried to give 'er some. I told 'er it were ma savin's, but she din't believe me. I mean, I guess I am a prostitute technically, but not in the way she thinks. When I go out dressed up an' meet men, it's coz I want to. Me an' Lady Die go on *walks* sometimes an' wait for guys to come up to us. Lady Die sez it's immoral to charge for doin' summat ya enjoy so much. Well, the stuff I charge for I don't enjoy, so ma conscience is clear. Mammar Joe don't know about any o' that, though. I sez, "I'm gonna move in wi' Pavash. Don't be upset." But she's worried about me livin' down town. I've told 'er I won't be doin' drugs or owt like that no more. Sez I just wanna be closer to college an' work.

One o' the saddest things I've learned workin' at Robin Hood Resorts is just how many old people are livin' on their own. One time I were phoning someone an' there were no answer, but I just lerrit ring an' ring coz I were tired an' cun' be bothered to dial the next number. But then someone picked up. She sounded dead old – in 'er eighties or summat – an' I felt awful coz I knew straight away she were no use to me, but I'd already disturbed 'er by that point. "Hang on," she guz. "Let me lower the television. I can't hear you." So I had to wait for 'er to shuffle off an' come back, knowin' it worra waste o' time for both of us. But I cun' hang up, could I? She said she din't remember fillin' in a questionnaire, but she seemed concerned, like she wanted to help. "My husband might have filled it in and put our names on. He died last year." So I asked 'er how long they'd bin together.

I felt so bad at first, coz I thought, I'm just wastin' this poor woman's time. But then I got the feelin' that she was happy to be talkin' to me. She told me 'er children don't visit very often so she spends most nights alone, in 'er chair, watchin' TV. I asked 'er what 'er favourite programmes was. What she'd had to eat that day. She thought I worra girl. Most people do on the phone. She asked me how old I am, an' if I'm courtin'. If I'd like to meet a nice man an' get married one day. Wear a big dress an' that. I laughed at that. She sez I could go abroad if I got married, me an' ma husband could go somewhere sunny for our honeymoon. She sez, "Would you like that?" No one could hear us, so I told 'er the truth. I sez, "Yeah, I would. I'd really like that, actually. One day."

I'm makin' so much money these days. I go out all night an' sleep all day. Like a vampire. No sneakin' out any more, though. It turns out Market Square toilets are open twenty-four hours an' ya can guess what guz on after midnight. I'm quite a hit there, I have to say. So I'm earnin' at Robin Hood Resorts in the evenin's, an' I'm earnin' at Market Square at night. Smanfa can't believe some o' the stuff I tell 'er, she thinks I'm makin' it up. Ya see, in 'er tiny little world, men'd never go wi' someone like me. I wish I had a hidden camera sometimes so I could show 'er what they're really like. Most people don't wanna know though, coz then they'd have to start questionin' their own lives. An' they don't wanna think it's *their* dads, *their* brothers, *their* boyfriends. But who do they think's payin' all these prostitutes? Santa? Just coz people don't talk about summat don't mean it's not happenin'. It is happenin'. It's happenin' all over the place. It's happening right now.

I'm just lookin' after mysen these days, fuck everyone else. Wi' the money I got wi' Liam, I've managed to save up a grand. Now, a thousand pounds really is a lot, innit? Makes Gaz's two grand seem a bit less impressive, eh? Coz I'm half 'is age an' I reckon I'm not doin' too bad. I love the fact I don't have to speak to 'im any more. I feel like I've bin waitin' ma whole life for this, but I know exactly how long it's bin, coz I broke the bathroom mirror the day I moved in. An' I remember thinkin', That's seven years' bad luck, coz I'm dead superstitious, me. I've got that off Mammar Joe. She won't go to bingo without 'er lucky bingo blobber an' she avoids cracks in the pavement. I have to break eggshells coz of 'er. She sez a witch might sail away in 'em if ya don't. I don't know why 'er bingo blobber's menna be lucky though coz it's hardly a medieval superstition, is it, bingo, but she swears by it. God knows what she'll do when it runs out. Probably just lose all the time.

But that mirror set the tone. An' everythin' I did from that day forward, includin' that, were wrong an' ma fault. I remember thinkin', It won't last for ever. But seven years feels like for ever when you're nine. Part of me actually thought I'd be able to go back to me mam's at some point. I spent every day for seven years wishin' I could go back to how things were, wishin' everythin' were different. I kinda got used to it in the end, but not really, not in ma heart. It just got worse an' worse as it became more an' more obvious that I'm not the first-born son Gaz wanted me to be. I tried ma best to hide it, but each year felt like I were menna be reachin' some new level of masculinity, an' each year I failed harder than the one before.

It's quite funny when ya think about it, though. Gaz Lees, the 'ardest man in 'ucknall – an' father to one of Nottingham's premier rent boys. I think he were hopin' for a footballer or summat. A boxer, like 'im. That's another thing. I don't have to go to another boxin' lesson for as long as I live. He tried to teach me to stick up for mysen, but it was ridiculous. I hated goin' with 'im, so in the end Uncle John said he'd take me instead. I love Uncle John an' enjoyed goin' with 'im more coz I've always wished he were ma dad, but I still hated boxin'. An' I still had to come home to Gaz. I hated every single minute I were there. Apart from the drives.

I could be mysen at me mam's. I could play wi' ma dolls an' ma Polly Pockets an' it were never a problem. I used to have Belle from *Beauty an' the Beast*, Princess Jasmine from *Aladdin*, an' Mulan. When I went to live wi' Gaz he made me put all ma girl's toys in a box an' took 'em off me. He said he'd dropped 'em off at the big Oxfam in Nottingham, so that weekend Mammar Joe took me. We asked if a box of dolls had bin handed in, but they said they'd not had owt like that. They were Christmas an' birthday presents, them dolls. Some of 'em were dead expensive. An' I honestly don't know what's worse – the thought of 'em sittin' in some skip, covered in muck, or thinkin' he gave 'em to one of 'is mates in Matlock, or wherever it is he guz when he's off to "see a man abaht a dog". Seven years later, an' I still wanna know. Are they in the corner of someone's bedroom? Maybe Paddy's little girl? Or Neil's? Or are they sittin' under a ton of rubbish somewhere? I'll never know.

If I can put up wi' 'im, I guess I can put up wi' Fag Ash. She was stayin' in a shelter for a bit but she's livin' with 'er cousin now in Sneinton. He's gay too. Fancy havin' two in one family – an' they're Muslims. Needless to say, they're the black sheep o' the family. I guess I am too. So I've taken their spare room. Ya can walk into town from here, so I basically go out for free these days. I gerra bottle of Cherry Lambrini an' drink it while I put ma makeup on, then head out. Sticky Nikki gets me into NG1 for free coz she works in the cloakroom now an' the doorman fancies 'er. So I don't have to pay for ma jacket or nuffin these days, an' we never pay for drinks. To be honest, I usually come back wi' more money than I go out with. People are always givin' me drinks or pills an' that. I've obviously got one o' them faces that sez, "Gizza line of coke."

Asha's dead tidy. Almost as bad as me mam. So that's good, coz I don't think I could live wi' someone who weren't. The house itself is a bit scruffy, but it'll do. There's no central heatin', but I've gorra wall heater in ma bedroom an' there's a gas fire in the livin' room, so I come down wi' me quilt wrapped round me in the mornin' an' we sit an' watch *Trisha*. They light candles when they have a bath, so I've started doin' it now an' all. I could never do stuff like that at Gaz's. He'd say that's what poofters do. An' it is. But the difference is, that don't matter here – coz it's tranny an' poof towers, an' we make our own rules. Asha's family forced 'er into an arranged married when she were eighteen. She's gorra little boy, but they don't let 'er see 'im now she's livin' as a girl. I can hear 'er cryin' at night sometimes.

The more I think about it, the more I appreciate how

nice it is to live somewhere where I'm not bein' constantly scrutinized an' judged for every little thing I say or do. It's like I can just, ya know, be mysen? An' no one bothers me. I'm so grateful I've not even argued wi' Fag Ash yet, an' I've bin here for a month. It's a miracle. I reckon she's bein' nice to me coz she likes the extra money. An' I'm dead clean. I've not invited me mam or anyone. I don't even know if I want 'em to know where I live, to be honest. I don't really like the fact Liam knows, but there's not much I can do about that. He an't bin round yet, thank God. I think he's avoidin' me as much as I'm avoidin' 'im. Good.

I've bin pretty worried about all that. Every time the door guz I keep expectin' it to be the police. At least it'd be here, an' not at Gaz's or Mammar Joe's. I even changed ma number coz I din't want Liam messagin' me, but it's pointless when he knows where I live. I've not had owt to do with 'im since ma psychosis. I don't even know why I did it now. Well, I do, an' it's pathetic. Coz I were scared. An' I wanted 'im to like me. To think I were cool. At least that's worrav bin tellin' mysen. But sometimes I lay in bed an' start thinkin', What if it's just coz I'm a massive twat? Coz I can't seem to stop doin' stupid stuff.

I've bin goin' out loads an' gerrin on it again too. When I'm off ma face is the only time I'm not worryin'. Ma "habits" have got worse too. I've bin washin' ma hands obsessively an' that sorta thing. I've got this new one now where I've gorra touch every bit of glass in the room before I can go to sleep. The windows. Ma mirror. Ma watch. It's weird, innit? Fag Ash sez I've got Obsessive Compulsive Disorder, but I don't see 'er complainin' when I'm on all fours cleanin' the oven out. I've gorra enrol at college soon. I've got enough GCSEs, just about. I'm shittin' it, but at least I did well in English – I gorran A! I'm gonna apply to Clarendon College. I've gorra try an' sort mysen out. I'm clever. I can't be a rent girl for the rest of ma life, canna? The problem is, I may have got mysen into a bit more trouble. I know. It's not even bin a month. But ya know worram like.

Lady Die wanted a piss. She sez, "Here, hold this", an' giz me 'er handbag. I were like, "Can't ya just wait till we get home? We were by the path at the top o' the Forest, just off Mansfield Road. I din't even see the guy till he were right next to me, he just come up an' went, "Excuse me, have ya got –" an' the next thing I know he's snatched ma bag out ma hand! Just swiped it off me. He snapped the handle an' all the beads went flyin'. So I were just stood there wi' this scrap of leather left in ma, tryna process what'd just happened. An' I just sort o' threw Die's bag at 'er an' razzed after 'im.

All I could think was, He's got ma phone, he's got ma bastard fuckin' phone – an' ma Laura Mercier makeup compact – an' I am *not* losin' another fuckin' phone. I'm always losin' ma phone. An' this is the *second* fuckin' time this has happened to me! The first time I were mugged I ran after 'im an' shouted, "Stop, thief!" like they do on telly, but there were no one about an' he were too fast for me. So I thought, Over ma dead body am I gonna let someone get away wi' muggin' me again.

Runnin'. It's the only physical activity I liked at school. Coz I've got long legs an' cross country's summat ya can do on yer own. I bet he assumed I were wearin' heels, but I had ma flip-flops on. I din't have any problems catchin' up with 'im, though. All I could think was, I've gorra catch 'im, I've gorra catch 'im, but as I started to close in on 'im I were like, OK now what? An' these flip-flops are goin' slap, slap, slap! Like someone bashin' one out. Lady Die's screamin', "Oi!" an' I'm lookin' at 'is shoes thinkin', I wish I had trainers on – an' then I have a brainwave. I think, I'll trip 'im up! So I swing ma leg an' catch 'is ankle, an' he comes crashin' down. I manage to get on top of 'im an' grab 'old of 'is wrists. He's on 'is back. I push 'is arms above 'is 'ead an' I'm in 'is face like, "Yes, ya little cunt, I've got ya now", but I'm worried he's gonna push me off an' beat me up, so I shout, "Die! Get here now!"

She's a bit behind us as she were mid-piss when it happened, but then she comes runnin' down an' I'm just prayin', Please get here fast, coz he starts strugglin' an' I'm worried he's gonna overpower me. But I'm thinkin', Am I fuck lettin' ya go. She finally catches up an' I'm like, "Sit on 'is legs!" cos he's thrashin' about. I look at 'im an' go, "Don't worry, she's used to dealin' wi' men's lower halves – yer in good hands." An' we just sat there on 'im till he stopped strugglin'. I sez, "Get yer phone out an' call the police. But *don't* let 'im get away."

He started strugglin' again though, so I got 'is wrists an' scraped the back of 'is hands across the gravel. I got in 'is face like, "Thought you'd mug us while we were vulnerable, din't ya? Well, guess what, ya picked the wrong girls, mate!" I'm thinkin', Maybe them boxin' lessons weren't such a waste of time after all. We stay like that for five minutes till the police come. Lady Die's cussin' 'im out, "Ya jankrow fucker." They were pretty quick, but it's a long time to be straddlin' a stranger. He were beggin' us to let 'im go, but I sez, "No, sorry, too late." He were foreign. I do feel a bit sorry for 'im, though, coz ya don't know where they've come from or what sorta life they've had, do ya? Coulda bin a war-torn country or summat. But I'm just so sick of people robbin' me.

I'm not kiddin', about five police cars turned up. I'm no fan o' the pigs but they did actually come to our rescue. The headlights were so bright. We must have looked funny, but I don't think they knew we were transsexuals coz one of 'em sez, "I bet he were lovin' it, wi' you two sat on top of 'im." He kissed Lady Die in the interview room! She's goin' on a date with 'im next week. I'm so jealous. I wish a fit police officer would kiss me. How does she always manage to pull people in the most unlikely situations? She din't even wanna go to the station at first, she were goin', "I can't be arsed to make a statement." She hates havin' owt to do wi' the police usually, so it's quite a turnaround really.

MS. JACKSON

Liam called me the other day. Fag Ash gave 'im ma new number. I'm pissed off coz she knows I'm tryna keep away from 'im, but I just styled it out an' were like, "Hiya, Liam, ya alright?" He said he were in a bit of trouble an' needed ma help. Sez this lad he's seein's bin accused of murder. Sez he's 'is alibi. But coz it's so serious the police need to confirm every detail. I were like, "Erm, OK." He sez, "It were that night." I'm like, "What d'ya mean, that night?" He guz, *That night*. Ah need ya to tell the pigs ya were wi' me, an' that ya saw me leave in a taxi." I'm thinkin', Are you fuckin' real? He guz, "Ah ordered it at half past twelve an' it come at quarter to one. I need ya to tell 'em ya were there an' had bin wi' me all night." I sez, "What about what we did?" He sez, "They don't know about that. So keep yer mouth shut, OK? Yer just confirmin' that I got in the taxi when I said I did, coz I got there at the time this murder is supposed to have happened. I need to prove he din't do it."

I reckon it's the one he's in love with. The one he plays that song about. One o' the Woodies. I really don't wanna talk to the police about what I were doin' that night, even if it's not connected, but I can't find a reason not to an' I don't wanna piss Liam off or get 'is mate in trouble. I did see 'im gerin a taxi at quarter to one, so I'd only be tellin' the truth. An' it seems to be important to 'im.

"But what if they ask us what we'd bin doin' all night?"

"Just tell 'em we'd bin playin' video games an' din't realize how late it was."

I go, "OK, Liam, I'll back ya up." An' regret it straight away. But what else can I do? When Liam asks ya to do summat, you do it – but that's how I landed in this mess in the first place, innit? The next day, I gerra phone call from the police. They ask me to confirm ma name an' address an' that I were wi' Liam Murphy on the night of January the twenty-fifth, two thousand an' three. I sez, "Yeah, I saw 'im leave in a taxi at quarter to one.' He guz, "OK, just to confirm, your legal name is Byron Lees, of 26 Finsbury Avenue, Sneinton, and you were at Flat 2, 34 Forest Road, Radford, on the night in question." I sez, "Yeah. That's right." He guz, "Thank you, that's very helpful."

"D'ya need anythin' else from me?"

"No, that's great. You'll be hearin' from us."

On Monday mornin' there worra knock on the door. Fag Ash were in the bath, so I answered. There were two policemen stood there. I sez, "Oh, how can I help ya?" I thought they'd come to gi' me an update on the guy who mugged me, but then one of 'em guz, "Are you Byron Lees?" I were like, "Yeah, is there a problem?" an' I'm shakin' by now coz I know it's bad. I can see people's net curtains twitchin' on the other side o' the road. You'd think they'd be used to police round here by

now. He guz, "I'm here to arrest you for unlawful impris-
onment and armed robbery. You have the right to remain
silent, but anything you do say may be taken down and
used against you in a court of law as evidence." It was
like what ya see on the telly an' that.

PORCELAIN

I hit a girl at school once. I can't even remember why now. I think we'd bin playin' tag an' she hit me, so I hit 'er back. I shun't have done it. I know I shun't. I'd not long moved in wi' Gaz an' school phoned 'im up. Just wait till yer father gets back. I sat there dreadin' 'im walking through the door, knowin' I had no escape. That house had an 'orrible vibe, it always felt so empty. One of ma earliest memories was goin' there an' lookin' up at the sunflowers by the jitty. An' that's where I stood waitin' for 'im, by the bins. I put every pair of pants I owned on to try an' soften the blow. Thirteen. I should've known it were bad luck. He felt 'em. He pulled ma jeans down an' sez, "Think yer clever, don't ya? Ah'll show ya who's fuckin' clever", an' whacked ma lower back instead. That's how I got the bruise.

'Is girlfriend Kelly lived there when I first moved in, an' she come out an' told 'im to leave me alone. They started arguing an' he chased inside after 'er. There worra lotta bangin'. I stayed where I were for what felt like hours, till finally he shouted, "Gerrin here, *now.*" There worra broken stereo at the bottom o' the stairs, but Kelly were long gone. She just took ma little sister an' left. They never come back.

I remember when I first come down wearin' ma

nightie. The fire had a grill round it to stop the dog an' the baby gerrin too close. Gaz was out, an' I sat there wi' ma fingers pokin' through the gaps, tryna get dry after ma bath. I wrapped ma hair up in a towel, like I've always done. An' Kelly looked at me like I were an alien, an' guz, "Why ya wearin' that?" No one on me mam's side o' the family had ever questioned me before, they just let me be mysen. I sez, "What d'ya mean?" She sez, "Girls wear nighties, not lads." I sez, "But I like wearin' a nightie." She sez, "I've got cousins yer age, an' they'd never wear that. Or sit there like that." I looked down at mysen an' thought, What's wrong with it? Why do I have to listen to this? I'm menna be at home. But that house weren't ma home. An' it were never OK to be mysen. Ya had to go through the back bedroom to get to the toilet an' she woke me up one time coz the door swung open an' the light come through. I were half asleep. But just as ma eyes were adjustin' she screamed, "Stop gawping!" an' slammed the door. I were like, What the fuck's just happened? But the fact is, she weren't comfortable wi' me. She din't want me there.

She always saw the worst in me. Things that weren't even there. They both did.

After she left, he blamed me. He resented me. He sez that if he hadn't have had to take me on, she'd have stayed an' he could've brought ma little sister up. Maybe he's right. Maybe if I hadn't have bin so out of control, I wun't have bin sent to live with 'im an' everyone would've bin better off. So I started goin' inside ma 'ead, fantasizin' about what I'd do when I grew up, about how I'd escape into the night, how I'd go to parties an' wear silver an' black. I thought I'd be free, one day, but yer never free, are ya? An' I'm laid here thinkin' about it – about all of it – coz this bloke's got the same stereo on 'is bedside table that were at the bottom o' the stairs that day.

I'm in Wolverhampton. I woke up on Sat'day mornin' an' got that feelin' in ma stomach that I always get before I do owt bad – like needin' to go to the toilet – an' thought, I'm goin' to Birmingham tonight. Lady Die an' Asha were bein' dry though, so I thought, Fuck it, I'll go by mysen. I din't wanna risk goin' out as a girl on ma own so I went to a gay club dressed as a boy. I met this lad on the stairs an' he gave me a Viagra. I sez, "What do I need that for?" But he reckons a lotta people take it to enhance their pleasure now, even women. So I went back with 'im an' we had sex till daylight. Then we slept for a bit. Then we had sex again.

By the time he dropped me off I were on a coke an' ecstasy comedown. My favourite. I'd told 'im I din't have any money to get home but he just went, "Ah, what ya gonna do?" I said, "I dunno." So he just left me at Wolverhampton, knowin' I had no way to get back. I thought, That's really fuckin' nice, innit, when you've spent all night wi' me, but who's to blame, eh? Me, as usual. Coz I'm a fuckin' twat an' I keep gerrin mysen into these ridiculous situations. It's bin six months since I were arrested, an' this is all I do now. I just go out. I don't go to college. Ma life's a mess.

I begged enough money in the station to get me back

to Birmingham, which ya have to go through anyway to get to Nottingham, an' thought I'll beg the rest there coz Birmingham New Street's dead busy. But by the time I get twenty quid, I'm hungry, aren't I? So I go an' buy a magazine an' a packet o' fags an' head to KFC. By the time I'd finished it'd got dark, an' I din't have enough money for a ticket, so I thought, I know what I'll do, I'll find some toilets. I cun' see any that were open though, so I just ended up walkin' around the streets for hours. Eventually I broke into a boarded-up buildin', an' just went an' lay down in the dark. It were dead peaceful, for a while. But then I heard sirens an' a car pullin' up, so I panicked an' ran out the back.

By the time I made it back to the station, the last trains were settin' off. I just sat down in the main corridor where the phone booths are an' waited. This black guy comes down an' I check 'im out on the sly – shaved head, proper muscular – but as he's walkin' off, he turns back an' looks at me, then looks up an' down the corridor, completely empty by that point. He sez, "Are yow alright?" In this 'orrible Brummie accent. They sound so thick! But he comes over. Asks me who I'm waitin' for. Ten minutes later, I'm smokin' a spliff in 'is sports car, bombin' about Spaghetti Junction. He's loaded.

He lives in a big house in the suburbs. Sez do I want some food, so I tell 'im I've not long eaten, but I could murder a bar o' chocolate. So he guz to fetch me a Snickers an' sez, "D'yow wanna shower?" I'm like, "Yeah, but I an't got no clean clothes, have I?" He sez, "D'yow want me to wash yer clothes? I've gorra dryer, they'll be ready by morning.' I'm thinkin', I've landed on ma feet here! But as I get out the shower, he's left a pair of silk shorts an' a T-shirt, an' I realize I'm basically trapped. But it's kind of hot. I go downstairs an' he's poured me a drink an' put porn on. I wanna go to sleep but I don't wanna offend 'im. We chat for a bit, but I'm yawnin' coz I'm absolutely knackered an' he sez, "D'yow wanna go to bed?" He follows me upstairs an' into the room I got changed in an' sez we can sleep here. But as I get into bed he locks the door. An' I know straight away I've got no choice.

He's downstairs now. An' I'm just layin' here, starin' at the stereo.

Alison sez I've bin "self-medicating". Alison's ma youth support worker. She's wi' the Youth Offending Team, which helps ya prepare for court if yer under eighteen. She's the one who's bin helpin' me get character references for Judge Thompson. He thinks I'm a piece of shit, ya can just tell. 'Orrible old bastard. The YOT do counsellin' an' help ya find clothes for court. I've even done acupuncture with 'em, to help wi' ma anxiety. Alison's dead nice. She thinks I've bin tryna stop feelin' things, an' she's right, coz the only time I'm not worried about goin' to prison is when I'm absolutely off ma tits. But it's not fun any more. It's not bin fun for a long time.

They don't have owt in police cells, not even a blanket in case ya rip it up an' try an' strangle yersen. They take yer belt an' yer shoelaces an' everythin'. They won't even let ya have a book, coz I begged the officer who was on duty to find me one. The lasagne were good, though. They're just frozen ones they put in the microwave, but they're actually quite tasty, coz ya can't go wrong wi' lasagne, can ya? Ya can't smoke though. I had to go to court the next mornin' an' I've never wanted a fag more in ma entire life. It were the magistrates for the bail hearin', but it'll be the Crown when I'm sentenced. That's where they deal wi' the serious crimes. That's where they deal wi' people like me.

Lady Die's come to court wi' me. Smanfa an' Sticky Nikki too, even Fag Ash has turned up, an' Dirty D. All the Fallen Divas. I told Mam, Aunty Ray an' Mammar Joe not to bother. I din't want 'em to see me upset. An' I din't wanna see them upset, coz that'd just make me even worse. I've given Smanfa me mam's number in case it's bad news, but she keeps sayin', "They're not gonna send ya down!" Apart from 'er, I'm not sure I've seen any of 'em out an' about this early, unless we've bin up from the night before. I go, "What an honour, seein' all these creatures o' the night in the cold light of day. Funny-lookin' things, aren't ya?" an' nudge Die in the ribs. "Especially you." She sez, "All this just coz ya got *dickmatized* by Liam. Stupid white bitch!"

We look different in the daylight. Smaller. I'm touched, truth told. There's summat about seein' a bunch of people who – Smanfa excluded – can barely even remember to brush their own teeth every day turnin' up to support a fellow Fallen Diva. Coz it means they're not just goin'-out mates. They're proper mates. We gorra photo in the passport booth on the way. We're idiots, aren't we? Fag Ash sez she's gonna get 'Free Paris' T-shirts printed if I get sent down, like when Deirdre got sent down on. *Coronation Street.* I think part of her's secretly hopin' I do coz she'll love the attention. I told Peter not to come. I just wun't have felt right with 'im here. I don't know why, I just don't want any grown-ups here. I feel ashamed. But it don't matter what Lady Die an' Smanfa thinks, does it?

Ma solicitor's here. She's not exactly fillin' me with hope, but they have to hedge their bets, I s'pose. They don't wanna get yer hopes up in case it's not the outcome ya want an' ya blame them. Better to lower yer expectations, innit, coz if it guz better than expected, it makes them look good. I feel like I'm in a film. Except it's real, innit? Ma barrister's like, "You know Judge Thompson was the subject of a BBC documentary last week?" I do coz I watched it at Peter's. Victims had bin sayin' 'is sentences were too lenient. She sez, "I don't want to upset you, but I'm afraid it's not looking good. Every person he's sentenced this morning has received at least two years." I sez, "Oh right. Thanks for lettin' me know."

But d'ya know what the real piss-take is? I were supposed to be sentenced a year ago! Coz I've bin turnin' up to court, unlike ma co-accused, dear old Liam Murphy. He's missed it three times now. They reckon he might be in Ireland, coz he's got family there. Judge Thompson had bin insistin' that we be sentenced together, but it's gerrin ridiculous now, so he's gonna sentence me either way today. Liam's nowhere to be seen again, of course. It's a shame, coz I'd love to see that smile wiped off 'is face. But no worries, babe, I'll just go to prison for the crime we committed on ma own, eh? Cheers, ya fuckin' cunt.

I just hope ma letters go in ma favour. I've submitted not one, not two, but three statements from respectable people vouchin' for ma good character. Even I were surprised I know three respectable people, let alone ones that'll vouch for me, but there ya go. Ma tutor said what a "bright and engaged student" I were an' how I should be in college, not wastin' ma time in prison. Everyone's bin tellin' me for the past six months, "They won't send *you* down!" but that's easy to say when it's not *their* necks on the line. The truth is, only Judge Thompson knows what turn ma life's about to take. An' very soon he's gonna let me know.

Nottingham Crown Court is opposite Broadmarsh bus station, an' if ya sit on the steps at the front an' look up to the right, ya can see the church at the top o' the Lace Market. It's bin converted to a bar called the Pitcher & Piano. Me an' Lady Die have had some bangin' nights in there. They play electroclash an' it's full o' the sorta girls who get their hair done at Toni & Guy, an' the sorta guys who wear shirts from All Saints. Beyond that's the Galleries of Justice, where the courts used to be in Olden Times. An' beneath all of it – beneath the court itself, no doubt – are the caves of Nottingham. They run for miles underground, a labyrinth of cold, dark tunnels. An' I'm sittin' on those steps now, smokin' a fag. I told them lot I needed five minutes.

It's stupid coz I've lived here all ma life, an' I've never really paid any attention to this buildin', an' I must have passed it so many times over the years. I pay attention to everythin', but I guess there's a lotta stuff ya don't even notice ya don't notice. Must have bin someone's idea of a joke buildin' a court in front of a bus station. I s'pose it makes it easier for all the scumbags to get here, eh? Scumbags like me. If I'm honest, I really don't like who I've become over the past few years.

An' I've never, ever wanted anythin' more in ma entire life than to get on one o' them buses an' just piss off somewhere. I wun't even care where it were goin'. Coz it's like standin' on the edge o' that wall, innit? It'd be the simplest thing in the world, but it'd change everythin'. I could just walk up to that bus, over there, an' go to Beeston. Or Eastwood. Or Arnold. I could look out the window at the trees an' the people on the streets, an' I'd be OK, even if only for today. I could go an' buy a cob, gerra cuppa tea, sit in the park – an' I wun't have to go to prison today. An' I bet if I were dead clever, I could escape the police for ages. Months. Maybe even years. I could change ma name an' move away an' maybe – just maybe – I'd get away with it. Just look how long Liam's gone without gerrin tracked down. An' I'm tempted. I'm so tempted.

An' I'm never gonna moan about waitin' for a bus ever again. Or traffic. Or havin' to stand. Coz people don't appreciate their freedom. An' it's only now, as mine's under threat, that I'm startin' to realize how much I've taken it for granted. Do all those people know how lucky they are to be on that bus? Alive, an' free. I wanna go up an' tell 'em. I wanna get on with 'em, just go far, far away. But I can't, canna? Coz if they din't get me today, they'd get me tomorrow. An' if not tomorrow, the day after. Months an' months could go by, an' I'd be runnin' the whole time, livin' in the shadows, always lookin' over ma shoulder. An' if – when – they got me, they'd throw the book at me. An' at the end o' the day, I'd deserve it. So I've gorra take responsibility for worrav done. I've gorra walk into that courtroom. I've never bin more scared in ma entire life.

I cun' even speak when they pulled us out the van. What got me the most was just how casual it all was. The guards. The cells. The cuffs. The prison van's like a bus, but instead of seats there's two rows of cells. They were playin' Britney Spears' new single on the radio. An' I just sat there, ma whole world fallin' apart, wi' two words goin' round ma 'ead: Two years. Two fuckin' years.

They put ya in a holdin' room at first. Ya know how there's always one dead bad kid at school that's bin excluded for hittin' a teacher or summat? Some proper little scumbag that ya'd run into movin' traffic to avoid? Well, yer shoved in a tiny room with about thirty of 'em, all showin' off an' intimidatin' anyone who looks weak. An' I'm thinkin', What the fuck am I gonna do? Coz I know the moment I open ma mouth it's all over. So I keep quiet, but it's no use coz they can smell the fear on ya, like Rottweilers. One of 'em guz, "What yo' in for?" So I mumble "Robbery" in the lowest voice I can an' he's like, "Ya don't look like a robber to me", an' I'm literally frozen wi' fear. He guz, "What d'ya rob – an old woman?" an' they all start laughin'. I'm gonna die in here. I know I am. They're either gonna kill me, or ma heart's just gonna explode, right now in ma fuckin' chest.

Then one of 'em's like, "Have ya got any burn on ya?"

an' I just look at 'im gone out. He guz, "Baccy? Tobacco? Fags?" I wish I did have a fuckin' cigarette. I'd smoke ten at once. I know deep down that a lot o' them must be shittin' it too, but at least they're actually who they're menna be. I doubt they've spent their whole lives feelin' like they're gonna get beaten up at any minute. Coz if I don't even feel safe walkin' down the street, how the fuck am I gonna survive here? For a year! A fuckin' year! One of 'em's lookin' through the slot in the door. He's mixed race, an' has an afro. He's gorriz hands down 'is pants, holdin' 'is balls. Why do they do that? He starts laughin', then shouts, "Are ya ready for a finger up yer arse, lads? Coz the screws 'ave got their gloves on!" That's gorra be a joke, right? Although, to be fair, a cavity search may be the one thing I'm prepared for in here.

I would do absolutely *anythin'* not to be in this room right now. I'd give all ma money. Not that I've got any, mind. I'd even be nice to Asha. Are ya listenin', God? Coz I promise to be good for the rest of ma life, if ya can please get me out of here. But it's too late, innit? Coz I've already done a deal, an't I? Wi' the devil. An' 'is name's Liam fuckin' Murphy.

Five hundred years later, an' two guards finally come an' open the door. One of 'em looks at 'is clipboard an' shouts, "Clifton, Robert!" an' a lad gets up an' leaves. A few o' the others look nervous, but most just look bored, like they're queuein' up at KFC or summat. I'm half expectin' one of 'em to ask why their fries are takin' so long. What I'd give to be in a KFC now. When they call ma name I'm like, this is it – this is ma moment. Ma perfect fuckin' moment. An' they send me into this reception area. There's loads more lads on the other side, crackin' jokes an' bein' cheeky wi' the guards an' that. Someone shouts "Oi, McKernan, ya bin sent down today?" An' another lad shouts, "Nah man, I've bin here since March. I'm just back from court." But then a guard pipes up, "The next person I catch shoutin' will be taken straight to the guv'nor." Some of 'em are sniggerin'. Maybe they're just frontin', but one thing I do know is, none of 'em look as scared as I feel. I'm not sure that would even be possible. I think it's fair to say I've got mysen into a bit of a fuckin' pickle here.

I'm shoved towards a desk where I have to say ma name an' empty ma pockets. I've gorra lighter an' a fiver. I gave ma phone to Smanfa. Further down the queue I can see they're makin' us take our clothes off. There's a screen, but it's not very private. I an't shaved ma legs for weeks coz I were worried this might 'appen, although I had hoped I'd bin bein' paranoid. An' I can hear Gaz in ma 'ead, an' Jamie Draper – all of 'em – goin', "Why d'ya talk like that? Why d'ya walk like that? Don't just stand there like a great big fuckin' poof." An' I just wanna smash ma 'ead against the wall.

Then they make me take ma clothes off. First the top half. Then the bottom. Ya have to stand wi' yer legs apart while they search ya, although it's over quicker than I thought it would be, thank God. The relief when they say ya can put your pants back on! An' the embarrassment when ya bend down for 'em! They don't put their fingers up yer bum – well, they din't wi' me, anyway.

But they take yer clothes an' gi' ya this 'orrible, prison-issue stuff to wear instead.

After that ya go down this corridor, but of course I take the wrong turn an' walk into a wall so the guard shouts at me an' I just go, "Sorry." I really, really do not wanna cry right now, but I can't help it, I can feel ma lip quiverin'. I bite ma tongue till I taste blood, but I can feel ma face scrunchin' up. Someone's gonna notice, but I can't stop it. A tear's comin' down. I put ma 'ead in ma hands.

One o' the guards sez, "Come on, it's not that bad." I can't even speak. I'm just shakin'. But the more I think about how freakin' out is only makin' things worse, the more I'm freakin' out. Like a vicious circle. What would Die do? Mam? Gaz'd be alright. I'd do owt to be like 'im right now. Some of 'em are pointin' at me an' laughin'. The guard sez, "Why are ya so upset?" I can't answer 'im. I don't even know. I can't even get through the reception. I'm the biggest fuckin' pussy in Notts, an' pretty soon the whole prison's gonna know it.

The guard mouths summat to one o' the other guards – the only woman here – an' she nods to summat behind us. Next thing I know he's takin' me by the arm an' sez, "Right, this way." I'm thinkin', Please don't let me be in trouble. But he ushers me into a side room an' sez, "What's the matter?" So I tell 'im, "I'm not cut out for this", an' he's like, "It's a prison. Yer not meant to enjoy it.' But he takes me to the hospital wing. I feel so relieved. Humiliated, yes. But mainly relieved. I'm so glad to be away from the others, I cun' give a flyin' fuck about ma pride. Maybe I can just keep shittin' mysen, so they lock me up on ma own, like a lunatic.

They put me in a room wi' two beds fixed to the middle o' the floor, the better to keep an eye on me, by the looks of it. There's a small glass window at the top o' the door an' every so often ya see a shadow an' a pair of eyes appear. I can't stop cryin'. They must think I'm mental. Maybe I am. I think this might just be the thing that tips me over the edge. No one else is sobbin' like this. I honestly think I might have to kill mysen. I can't face a whole year of bein' bullied in here. I just cannot do it. I don't have the physical or mental strength.

The nurse comes in an' guz, "Still not eaten? You'll feel better if you can get some food down you." They gave me a sandwich an' a packet of crisps when I got here, but I can't eat. I tell 'er I'm sorry, I've already bin sick once, an' I ask 'er if it's normal for people to get this upset. She sez, "It does happen. But yes, you are very upset", an' asks me worram most worried about. So I tell 'er, "I'm a girl on the outside. An' I can't hide it. I can't change the way I talk. I sound gay. Everyone's gonna know straight away." I beg 'er not to send me back wi' them lads.

She sez I can stay on the hospital wing till I calm down a bit. I ask 'er if she can gimme summat for ma nerves, but she sez they only gi' tablets out in extreme circumstances an' the doctor has to sign it off. "Do you feel suicidal?" she guz. An' in all honesty, I do. I just wanna stop feelin' like this, an' I don't see how I can ever *not* feel like this so long as I'm in here. She sez they might put me on a special unit for vulnerable prisoners, an' to try an' get some sleep. I always thought it worra turn of phrase when people say, "I cried mysen to sleep", coz how can ya fall asleep if yer cryin'? But ya can. I tossed an' turned all night. Light was comin' through the gaps round the door. When I closed ma eyes, I could see demons writhin' around on the ceilin', snarlin' at me, growlin', hissin'. The only thing worse was wakin' up.

LONELINESS

Ever seen *Scum*? "The film they tried to ban", accordin'
to the cover. Ray Winstone's in borstal an' he beats this
lad up an' guz, "I'm the daddy now." Gaz had it on VHS.
He made me watch it when I went to live with 'im. I
reckon he was tryna put me off bum sex, coz there's this
scene in it where they rape one of 'em in the greenhouse.
It's absolutely horrendous. I remember thinkin', Why's
he showin' me this? I must've bin about ten or eleven.
Well anyway, that's how it is in here. OK, no one's raped
me. An', to be fair, no one's whacked me round the 'ead
with a snooker ball wrapped in a sock an' told me they're
the daddy, either – but the clothes, the screws, the food,
it's all just as 'orrible as you'd expect.

But weirdly, at the same time, it's not actually as bad as
I thought it'd be. Coz when I first got here, it felt like I'd
just bin dropped off at the gates of hell. An' don't get me
wrong, it is truly vile. But I've bin here a week now an'
I'm still – how can I put it? Alive. I felt like I were gonna
die that first day. It were just this overwhelmin' sense of
dread. Feelin' like I cun' cope. But it's a paradox, coz
even though I hate every second, the flipside is that every
minute that passes feels like a major achievement. Every
mornin' I wake up an' remember I'm here. An' it's awful.
But I also know I'm one day closer to gerrin out.

I were sentenced on the Friday. I cried for the first twenty-four hours, but I managed to calm down a bit by Sunday. They're gonna put me on Unit Five, for vulnerable prisoners. I'm worried it's gonna be full of nutcases, but I'd rather that than be wi' them lads I were dropped off with. I've gorra spend a week on Unit Fifteen first though. The induction wing. So that's where I am. They asked me if I were gay at dinner today. I just froze, so they must be on to me now. They open the doors an' let ya come out to socialize once a day, but I just stayed inside after that. I don't even wanna go out for food, to be honest. It's like bein' back at school, but worse. I an't cried today though, so that's summat.

It takes a few days for 'em to process yer information but I should get money added to ma canteen tomorrow, which means I can phone people an' buy tobacco. I would really, really, really like a cigarette right now. I don't think I've ever wanted owt more in ma entire life. It's the longest I've bin without one. I should get ma release date soon too. If ya get two years, ya only do one inside. The second year's called probation, which means yer free, but they can send ya back if ya get in any more trouble. So ma release date'll be next January, but I want the exact date so I can start countin' down the days. They've given me a diary wi' quotes from the Bible in it, so I cross off every day I'm here. Maybe I'll turn to God.

But what I *really* want, even more than a fag, is ma HDC date. Home Detention Curfew. They put a tag on ya, an' ya have to be home by a certain time. Like six o'clock or summat. So if I gerrit – an' I have to gerrit –

it's about a third of yer sentence, or a third of what ya would spend in prison. Basically it means I could get out of here four months sooner if I behave mysen. The best-case scenario, then – the earliest possible opportunity that I'll be leavin' here – is in eight months. I can't even get ma 'ead around it, to be honest. I already feel like I've bin here eight weeks, an' it's not even bin eight days. But what can I do?

I probably shun't get ma hopes up, but I can't help it. I don't care worrit takes, I have to get HDC. Apparently, not everyone gets offered it, but it's the only thing that's keepin' me goin'. I've gorra be the most feminine person to have seen the inside of Glen Parva Young Offenders Institution. It's not very Joan Collins, is it, borstal? They've put me in a cell on ma own. I've gorra TV. I watched *Poltergeist* on ma first night on this wing. Ya hear people goin' on about how they shun't have TVs in prison an' that, how "it's like a holiday for 'em". Well, I'm not bein' funny, but if I paid for a holiday an' ended up here I'd be writin' a very strongly worded letter to Thomas Cook.

I'm glad I told everyone straight away. Coz I can't pretend the whole time. I wish I could, but I tried to pretend I'm normal for seven years, an' it din't work. I've toned it down a bit – I've gorra voice I'm doin' to sound a bit more like the others, but I feel like such a freak. It's like goin' to Ireland an' tryna pretend I'm Irish or summat. It's just not gonna wash, is it?

SEE IT IN A BOY'S EYES

Unit Five. Where they put all the paedophiles, or so they say. There's one or two I wun't put it past, but most of 'em are just normal lads, not what ya think of when ya think o' criminals. One of 'em's in here coz he ran some-one over when he were drink drivin'. I feel a bit sorry for 'im coz he clearly don't belong in here, but I guess he shun't have done it at the end o' the day. He were comin' back from a party. It's easily done, innit?

I've told everyone I'm queer. I just cun' deal with it. They'd have bin askin' me about it within a few days any-way, an' I just cun' cope wi' the pressure, or bein' interrogated like I were at school, all over again. Maybe there's someone better than me who'd be able to hide it, but I just can't. No one went mental or owt, it was like they were too shocked to even take the piss. I reckon some of 'em thought it worra joke. But the next day, people started bein' funny wi' me. I went outside to smoke durin' association an' I were shockin' 'em wi' ma crudeness. I don't think they know what to make of me yet. I'm sure I'll win 'em over. I'll find a way to make 'em laugh.

To be honest, I've bin feelin' much better since I gorra letter from Max. He come up to the prison wi' Lady Die an' tried to see me but they wun't let 'im in. The screws say I've gorra send 'im a Visitin' Order first. Screw is what they call the guards – coz they screw ya over, I guess. Max sez he loves me! An' he's sorry how everythin's turned out. Sez he'll come an' see me, an' that he'll be waitin' for me when I come out. Sez he wishes it could all have bin different. So do I. Well, maybe it can one day.

I got ma HDC date too. Tenth of September. If I'm accepted for it. Please God, gimme the strength to get through this. I can't spend Christmas in here. That's one of ma worst fears, bein' in an institution at Christmas. When I were dead naughty when I were little, Mam always used to say they'd come an' take me away an' I'd have to live with other naughty kids "So you'd best behave". I've seen 'em on telly, "homes" for delinquents. They lock the doors an' that, they're like prisons. An' I were terrified of bein' taken from ma family an' put in one o' them homes. An' now look at me. I'm officially a delinquent. I've got the T-shirt an' the stint in borstal to prove it. They don't really call 'em borstals any more. They're called young offenders institutions now. But that's about the only thing that looks like it's changed here in the past thirty years.

Lady Die sez she's gonna be dead bored without me. Good. I want everyone to be dead bored without me. I want the whole friggin' world to just stop, actually. But it won't, will it? Coz they were playin' all the new songs on the radio today an' it got me thinkin', Everythin's just gonna carry on as normal. The bin men'll still be out this mornin'. Mam'll still be catchin' 'er bus. Lady Die'll still be a fuckin' slag. There'll be traffic jams, an' parties,

177

an' special offers in 'Tescos, an' life'll just carry on without me. Coz I know it sounds stupid, but I've just realized
I'm not actually the centre o' the fuckin' universe. An'
it's got me thinkin' about when I die. Coz yeah, people'll
be upset for a while. An' they'll go to ma funeral an' cry,
an' me mam might be depressed for a bit an' take time
off work. But in the end, they'd all just carry on, eh? Coz
I'm the only person ma life really matters to. An' I've
fucked it up. Big time.

ERASE/REWIND

It feels like the ceilin's pressin' down on me. I'm lyin' in bed. It's like it's closin' in, like one o' them machines that crush cars. I keep thinkin' about where I am. I don't mean here, in prison. I mean ma place, in the world. An' how low I've sunk. One of ma favourite books when I were little were called *Cops an' Robbers*. I've still gorrit somewhere. I remember it off by heart:

> Here are the cops of London town
> In the station at half-past two.
> They drink their beer
> And raise a cheer
> For upstanding Officer Pugh.

> Here are the robbers of London town
> In cells all gloomy and grim.
> "Let us out, let us out!
> Not guilty!" they shout,
> And, "It wasn't me – it was him!"

> Ho Ho for the robbers
> The cops an' the robbers Ho Ho!

I always hated Officer Pugh. I wanted the robbers to escape. There's a scene where he wrestles one of 'em to the ground an' arrests 'im, an' I wanted 'im to throw 'im off an' run away. There's two pictures that I absolutely love in it though, the first one an' the last one. The first one shows the police station cut in half. Ya can see all the floors, like a doll's house. The police are havin' a party, drinkin' wine an' eatin' cake. It's Christmas an' they're wearin' silly hats. Below, in the cells underneath the station, all the robbers are sittin' on their own, lookin' miserable an' lonely. An' sittin' here, in this cell, all gloomy an' grim, I can see that picture like it's in front of me. The lines goin' over an' over in ma 'ead:

> Ho Ho for the robbers
> The cops an' the robbers Ho Ho!

An' I start thinkin' about this poster we had in home economics that showed ya how much ya should be eatin' of all the different types o' food. All the stuff yer not supposed to eat's at the top – so all the nice stuff, like sweets an' chocolate – an' at the bottom's all the stuff yer menna get lots of, like fruit an' veg. But in ma version, at the top o' the pyramid is all the most important people. So the Queen's at the top, an' then as ya go down there's like lords an' ladies an' that, then judges an' celebrities. Joan Collins is quite near the top. Then ya have the bank managers, an' the mayors, an' it keeps goin' down, wi' more people the further ya go. Police officers. Builders. Bin men. All gerrin less an' less important, till ya get to all the homeless people, all the drug dealers an' the prostitutes. An' then, right at the bottom, in the dirt, you've got everyone who's bin sent to prison. The murderers. The rapists. The robbers.

Ho Ho for the robbers
The cops an' the robbers Ho Ho!

An' I keep thinkin', How have I got here? How am I at the bottom o' the pyramid? An' I'm terrified there's no way back up. The more I think about it, the more I feel like the ceilin's about to collapse on me. I feel trapped. I am trapped! Coz where would I go? I'm worried that if I take ma eyes off it for a second, it'll come crashin' down an' I'll be crushed under the weight of it. So I sit here, lookin' for cracks in the plaster. An' I keep askin' mysen, "How did ya get here? How did ya end up in a prison cell? On a prison-issue mattress? An' with a prison-issue blanket? Starin' up at a prison ceilin'?" An' every time, I've only got one answer: I fucked up.

Coz I can make all the excuses I like, but if yer restin' yer 'ead on a prison-issue pillow – unless there's bin some huge miscarriage of justice – ya kind of have to accept you've made some pretty bad decisions. So that's worrav gorra do. Accept the fact I've made some big mistakes. Coz I *am* here, under a prison-issue blanket, on a prison-issue mattress, lookin' up at a prison ceilin', an' it's not a nightmare, sadly. It's ma life. I robbed someone. I committed a crime. An' now I'm doin' the time. But what's next?

Ho Ho for the robbers
The cops an' the robbers Ho Ho!

In *Cops an' Robbers*, Officer Pugh catches all the robbers an' throws 'em in the cells. Obviously. It's Christmas

Eve an' it's bin snowin'. Everywhere's white. All the kids who've bin robbed get their stolen presents back in time for Christmas. There's a picture of 'em all tucked up in bed, dreamin' of Santa. They live in nice, cosy houses, an' their mams an' dads have put trees up an' covered 'em wi' tinsel. The robbers all get their comeuppance. All of 'em except one, that is. Coz on the last page we find out what happens to ma favourite character:

> And the toys? Oh, they were taken back
> By a Santa Claus copper with a Santa Claus sack.
> While the rest of the force searched day and night
> For an elderly lady of medium height
> With a fondness for earrings and red fox furs
> And a habit of taking what wasn't hers.
> She usually carried a sizeable bag;
> Her name, of course, was Grandma Swagg.
>
> Ho Ho for the robbers
> The cops an' the robbers Ho Ho!

There's a picture of a crowd gathered round a wanted poster wi' Grandma Swagg's face on it, but she's right there, at the back, hidin' in plain sight. She's wearin' a stripy top an' a dead fox round 'er neck. No one sees 'er coz they're all too busy lookin' at the poster. I loved that as a kid. But d'ya know what's really pathetic? Deep down, I always thought I were Grandma Swagg. That I could do whatever I wanted, an' that I wun't get caught. Coz although I stand out everywhere I go, I guess I've never really felt like anyone can see me.

PURE SHORES

Mam's written me a letter:

43 Ragdale Close
Hucknall
Nottinghamshire
NG15 6YB

Dear Byron

I am sorry that I have kept missing your phone calls. If you ever ring me and I don't answer leave me a message letting me know when you will next ring and the time and I will sit by the phone and work around it. I have rung Glen Parva nearly every day but they tell me they can't give me any info and can't pass on a message to you. They put me through to the chaplain's office but it keeps ringing and there is no answer or answer machine. I hope you are OK and want you to know I am always thinking of you and wish we could have met and sorted things out before you went away. I would like to come and see you so please send me a visitors' pass and explain how I can get in touch with you. Do you need anything? Clothes, books, fags, phonecard? Please let me know and I will get it to you.

The reason I have the address and know where you are is because me and Bobby were having lunch at the Pilgrim and

when we had eaten Deon and his friend came over. They intro-
duced themselves and asked if I was your mum. I was quite
surprised and I thought I recognized Deon's friend's face. I looked
at him and said "Haven't I seen you somewhere before?" It was
Max! I thought it was him. He let me copy the address off a letter
he was sending to you. I am glad that they are both supporting
you and I really appreciate them coming over. Bobby thought they
were really nice lads. I wish I had asked them to join us for a
drink now, but I was a bit surprised at the time. Max looked
really nice and better-looking than all those years ago.

You won't believe the next bit. It was Mammar Joe's birthday
on Wed last week so I asked her what she wanted to do, and you
can guess what, can't you? She wanted to go to Gala Bingo. It was
really bad weather and very icy so Bobby drove me to Gala. (We
have a car now. It's a Honda CR-V silver. It's a bit like a Free-
lander jeep but trendy.) Met Mammar Joe & Aunty Ray in the
foyer and I thought I saw Max walk by. Well, it turns out that
he was working there. He was the bingo caller for the evening and
he has a lovely voice. Told Aunty Ray who he was and we all
thought he seems like a really nice person. Mammar Joe actually
won £70 which she made me & Aunty Ray share with her. I
actually had 2 lines at one point but didn't realize it and by the
time Mammar Joe shouted Bingo for me someone else had won. I
couldn't concentrate cos Mammar Joe was talking all the time! I
bought her a Hoover for her birthday and sent a bouquet of
flowers to her work. She really liked that, being one of those
women who have someone send flowers to them at work.

Sorry if this letter is untidy but I just want to get it out as if I
am talking to you. I'm not very good at writing letters but I will
be doing a few now. Watched a Panthers match at the Ice Stadium

last night. I arranged for work to sponsor the evening match. We had our own executive box with waitress service and I got to present to the winner. They took my photo and it will be in next week's programme. I will send you one when it is published!

Bobby told me you would ring Monday but I am at work so if I don't manage to pick it up keep trying. Your dad came round to see us as he was worried about you and I gave him the address. He said he wouldn't write but wants to see you. That's your decision to make but try and give Mammar Rita a ring cos she is worried about you. Please write to me soon if you can and remember I love you. What's happened has happened. You can't change the past, you can only move forward. I changed my life late on. Now you've got a head start on me so choose what life you want to have. I will love you anyway!

Mam xxxx

Well, that's nice that Max has finally got 'er blessin', innit? Two years too late an' I'm in fuckin' prison, but thanks very much, Lisa. Although it is quite sweet, if I'm honest, so I've written back to 'er. I can't remember writin' to someone I actually know before. Like, I had to do an application letter for college, an' a coverin' letter for ma CV, but this is like proper Olden Times, innit? I've decided to write it in proper English coz the screws read yer letters before they post 'em. You're not allowed to seal the envelope. I think it's so ya don't plan an escape or summat. I don't want 'em thinkin' I'm common so I've gorra copy of *Pride an' Prejudice* from the library an' I've used it as a guide. I read the whole thing in two days. It's like ya can escape when ya read. I'm readin' *The Picture of Dorian Gray* now. They locked 'im up, din't they, Oscar Wilde? I saw a thing once where he'd said he'd bin born in the wrong century. Well, I don't know when the right one's menna be comin' coz the twentieth left a lot to be desired, an' the twenty-first's not looking any better from where I'm standin'. But at least I'm in prison for doin' summat wrong. Oscar Wilde's only crime were bein' gay.

Here's worram sendin' back:

When writing to Members of Parliament please give your previous home address in order to avoid delay in your case being taken up by the M.P.

In replying to this letter, please
write on the envelope:
Number: MA4221
Name: LEES
Wing: 5

Dear Mother,

Don't worry about missing my phone calls, I can only use the phone here at certain times. I have run out of credit now so I won't be able to phone you for about a week, but I will leave you a message as requested if you don't answer. It's no good trying to ring me, so don't waste your time.

I was very pleased to receive your letter, it is comforting to know you are thinking about me. I understand that you must be quite worried about me, but as dear Mammar Joe has probably told you, I am doing fine. I have been put on to Unit 5 and you will need to put this with the address, along with my number which is MA4221. This will ensure your letter gets to me as soon as possible. This unit is for vulnerable prisoners and there are some nice lads here. I have only been here for about a week.

It hasn't been as bad as what I thought it would be actually, and no one in here really seems to mind that much that I am gay, and some people even like me. I am gobsmacked as I didn't think anyone would even want to talk to me, but they do and I've had a right laugh some days!

I will be starting education soon which means I can get my A-levels completed and the certificates don't say anything about the course being in prison. It will also make the days go a bit faster. At the moment I am just watching TV and reading books all day. I have read Pride and Prejudice and From Russia with Love since I have been here. I am sure I will get excellent results in here as I am more than able, the only reason I didn't do well at college was due to the distractions of my lifestyle.

I hear what you are saying about wishing we had sorted things out before all this, but it is something we should have done anyway. I do feel that you do not put the same amount of effort into our relationship as you do with other areas of your life, and this is a consistent fault with our past relationship. Even so I would be happy to see you, so I have enclosed a Visiting Order that will allow only you, Mammar Joe and Aunty Ray to come. You can tell Gaz that just because I have been sent down don't make us best mates all of a sudden. If he wants to start making things better he can begin by sending a letter apologizing for the many years of negative comments and hurt he has caused.

As for you, all I ask is for you to fully accept me. I don't ram this down your throat but if you do want a relationship with me *then the subject presents itself. I suggest you ask Mammar Joe to show you all my photos at the flat. If you don't like it then don't bother writing to me, but just remember that I am the product of your and Gary's efforts.*

I appreciate the offer of sending me cigarettes etc. but it is not allowed. What you can do however is send me envelopes so long as they have an address and stamp on them. It would be helpful if everyone could do that, it would be one less thing that I have to pay for. I would be grateful for some pants and socks as well. Just a couple of each. You may need to ring and check how you go about this. If you are feeling particularly generous and sorry for me then would you give my friend Samantha some money to buy me some new trainers to bring me? Perhaps you could arrange to meet her in town. Her home number is 9520604. It's just that I am wearing regulation horrible shoes, but my old ones aren't worth sending in as they are battered.

I'm pleased to hear about the new car and your evening at the Ice Stadium. Sounds like you were the lady of the evening. I'm also extremely pleased that you approve of Max, even though it is rather too late now. Anyway I've run out of space to go on about that, so all I can do is ask you to pass my love on to Aunty Ray and Mammar Joe and not to worry about me. Hope to hear from you soon and thank you for your letter.

Then I signed off. The thing about me mam is, she lets me down but she's not 'orrible like Gaz. She's just not a very good mam. But I do at least feel like she loves me. An' I love 'er too. I've got 'er, Mammar Joe an' Aunty Ray, so I count mysen lucky really. Some people don't have anyone.

SILENCE

Mam lives wi' Bobby now. She told me on the phone. An' she's fallen out with 'er best mate Denise, coz she tried it on with 'im! That's bad, innit? Apparently it's not the first time either, coz she flirted wi' Gaz outside the Station Hotel when they were younger. She were wearin' shorts an' put a fiver between 'er legs an' sez, "Come an' gerrit, then." While Mam were goin' out wi' 'im! She's gone absolutely mental this time coz she sez they're not kids any more an' Denise should know better. Mam's not jealous usually, but woe betide anyone who tries owt on with 'er man. Apparently she confronted Denise in the Wine Bar an' went, "But the best bit is, they both turned ya down – an' told me! They din't even want ya! But I guess ya weren't satisfied wi' bein' humiliated once." She sez she's never gonna speak to 'er again.

She told me ma great-grandad's died too.

Grandad George. I used to go an' see 'im after school. He'd go, "What ya brought for me?" At first I'd say summat like, "Just mysen, Grandad", but then I started takin' 'im packets of Jammy Dodgers, so I could say, "Will that do ya?" It always smelled o' cat food. He weren't like Gaz, I never heard 'im say a harsh word about anyone. He used to work down the pit, back when they'd come home covered in soot – God knows how they kept their houses clean. Apparently it were dead dangerous, a lot of 'em used to die down there. They got problems wi' their lungs too, but Grandad had a good innin's. He were eighty-one. He were born in the nineteen-twennies. That's like, Olden Times, innit? That's when *Lady Chatterley's Lover* is set. We did it at college. That's when 'er baby would've bin born.

No one on ma dad's side o' the family has contacted me. Mam told me she saw Mammar Rita on 'ucknall High Street an' she sez she wants to write to me, but she don't wanna upset me. Worra loada crap. I know exactly why they an't told me. They don't want me turnin' up an' ruinin' the funeral. Coz they'd let me out for a funeral. I'd have to have two screws wi' me though, an' wear handcuffs. Ya can't even take 'em off for the service. But I could go. I could physically be there. Can't say I blame 'em, to be honest, coz it is summat to be ashamed of, bein' in here. But it don't make no difference anyway. They've bin ashamed of me from the moment I could talk.

CHERRY LIPS

Mammar Joe's written back to me:

16A Sherwood Close
Hucknall
Notts
NG15 6BR

Dear Boo Boo!

Thank you for your letter, it was really nice to hear from you.

I am trying not to worry too much. Having the job helps immensely. I miss you and hope you are feeling alright. I am sure this time in your life will be positive, beneficial, and you will emerge with a sense of direction, as well as qualifications.

I know when I have done things I didn't particularly want to do or gone on a course I wasn't sure about I have always learned something from it.

I want you to be positive and keep in good spirits. Please hurry up and send me a visitors pass, and let me know if you need anything bringing, and phone me!

I love you and miss you.

Mama (a.k.a. Old Mother Hubbard!) xx
P.S. Guess who I saw on television this morning!

Anybody would think I were on an IT course. It's funny that she saw me on telly, though. Me an' Lady Die saw a sign in the newsagents askin' for people to come an' be in the audience for *Trisha*, so we signed up. They send a coach for everyone who's put their names down, so we had to meet at the Cash Shop just off Market Square. It's filmed in Norwich. I wore ma black an' green dress from H&M an' ma red wig. The one I nicked. I love that wig. An' I spoke! I made a comment an' gorra round of applause from the audience.

They film it dead far in advance, but they told us when our episode were gonna air an' I cun' believe it when they said it was goin' out a week after I were due to be sentenced. So on Tuesday, I sat here, in a young offenders institution for boys, in a cell wi' nowt in it but a television, a mattress an' a few books, an' watched mysen on telly for the first time. As a girl! I told everyone in here so they all know what I look like on the outside now. I'm gonna ask Mammar Joe to send me some photos when I speak to 'er so I can show people an' put 'em on the wall. I want 'em to see me.

I nicked some coloured chalk from art class yesterday an' crushed it into little piles of dust. Then I plucked ma eyebrows wi' ma nails. It took me ages, but it's not like I've got owt better to do, is it? When they turned the lights off, I used the chalk as makeup. We wun't be allowed a proper mirror in here coz it's glass an' yer not allowed owt that could be used as a weapon. But there's a piece of metal in the toilet that ya can use to see yersen in. I probably looked like shit, but in the dark, by the light o' the telly, I almost looked like me.

Had a bad night last night. I spoke to mam on the phone an' she told me Gaz is only two birthdays away from bein' forty, an' it just floored me coz I always forget how old people are. After I got into bed it got me thinkin' about Grandad, an' how time moves on. How me mam's gonna die. An' Aunty Ray. An' everyone I know. An' I just felt so small. It was like I were lookin' into this darkness that just went on an' on, for ever. Ma heart started racin' an' I cun' breath. I had to gerrout of bed in the end an' I just lay there, on the floor, an' held mysen. I cun' stop shakin'. I wanted to call for help, but what would I have told 'em? There was nowt wrong wi' me, although I kept thinkin', What if I die in here? What if I just drop dead? I felt so trapped. It was 'orrible.

I've bin thinkin' about Mammar Joe's letter an' she's gorra point. In fact, I've bin doin' a lotta thinkin' in here, an' I've gorra get ma act together. Coz this can't be ma story, can it? Mr Gallagher sez two-thirds of first-time offenders end up behind bars again within two years of bein' released. Mr Gallagher's ma favourite screw. He's from Glasgow an' he's the only one who talks to ya like yer not a piece o' shit. But that means most of us will be back here very soon. An' I do not like those odds. I don't like 'em one little bit. I've gorra get

HDC an' make sure I'm part o' that thirty-three point three three three per cent recurrin' or whatever it is that don't fuck up again.

Ya can buy *Gay Times* in here. I were dead happy when I saw they were selling that, coz I thought they'd just have *Loaded* an' that. An' I've bin thinkin' about how I wanna do good stuff when I'm back on the road, ya know, live like all them people ya read about in magazines. Coz assumin' I don't actually drop down dead, I've got ma whole life ahead of me. So I may as well make the most of it, eh? I shun't even be in here. I should be at college. I could be the first person in ma family to go to university. I've actually got the brains to do it, but I'm here, followin' in Gaz's footsteps. Lads like 'im can survive in places like this, they just go gym an' take the piss out of each other. But I'm not like 'im, no matter how much ma current situation suggests we're more similar than I'd care to admit.

All I've ever wanted is to grow up so I can do whatever I want, but look where it's landed me! I can't do fuck all. An' even when I can again, what good is it if I don't like who I've become? I can't even stop smokin'. I don't wanna be like Mammar Joe an' have bin on the fags for thirty-odd years by the time I'm fifty. I don't wanna hang around wi' the people I've bin hangin' round with. I've got some good people in ma life, but I've also got some really bad ones. It's an opportunity to start fresh when I come out. I wanna go back to college an' finish ma A-levels. I've gorra get a good job an' build a better life for mysen, coz I can't have sex for money for ever, canna?

An' I wanna be a girl. I can kid mysen on the outside, but the truth is I'm just not like the other lads in here. They know it, an' I know it. An' it's not about bein' "gay" either. There's a lad in education who's come out as bisexual now. Sez he's inspired by me. So that's nice. But it's not the same thing, I realize that now. Coz it's killin' me bein' in here an' not bein' able to express that side of mysen. I thought it were just a bit of fun. But it's not. It's deeper than that. It's about who I am.

I know there's no point feelin' sorry for mysen, but I've got so much time to think in here that I can't help it. But I just feel like everythin' would've bin different if I'd had a nice middle-class family, that talked how Peter an' people on TV do. I know I could hold ma own wi' people like that, I know I'm clever enough. Some o' the lads here don't have any options when they come out.

I kept hearin' this noise the other day. Knockin', followed by a whoosh, like a letter had bin slipped under ma door. But there were no screws about. I looked down an' it worra comb, with a bit o' string tied to it. Then this lad in the cell opposite shouts, "Ya got it?" He'd skimmed it across the corridor. I sez, "Why has it got string on it?" He guz, "So I can pull it back wi' the burn yer gonna lend me." I thought, Ya cheeky bastard, but I wanna make mates so I folded some up an' attached it. 'Is name's Jason. Brummie. Sez he's on tablets for depression. He don't have any family to go back to, just a bad crowd waitin' for 'im, by the sounds of it. Sez he was abused as a kid. Sez he knows he'll just start takin' smack again as soon as they let 'im out, an' that he'll end up back in here. Sez he prefers it to outside.

I know what he means. I spend all day thinkin' about how to get out of here. I come up with all these elaborate schemes, like goin' to the library an' pretendin' I'm someone else. Or tunnelling. Or knockin' out a screw an' stealin' their uniform. But when they turn the lights off, an' it gets quiet, ya can feel the radiators rattlin', an' it's relaxin'. Like when Gaz takes me for a drive. Coz ya don't have any control in here. Ya just have to accept that they're lookin' after ya. An' it's nice.

But it has to be ma last time. I can't be like Jason. I can't do this again. Coz I'm better than this, I know I am. I've got the potential to do well. An' options, when I'm back on the road. I wish I could help Jason, but I don't even know how to help mysen. It feels insurmountable. I found that word in a book the other day, an' it's exactly how I feel. Like I've got this great big mountain to climb. I've got this vision of who I could be, an' what ma life could be like. I keep thinkin' about this textbook we had in French. It had a picture on the cover of a group of teenagers. Three lads an' three girls, all tanned an' good-lookin'. They're on bikes, at a train station, but they've stopped to talk. It's summer an' they're all smilin'. All look dead relaxed. An' I must've sat an' stared at that picture for hours, wishin' I could be part o' their world. Coz I'd give owt to be like them. But I don't know how. I din't have a clue in school, an' I've got even less of one now.

I guess one o' the good things about bein' locked up is that I've got plenty o' time to try an' work it all out. Coz I may be at the bottom, but I've gorra start somewhere. Mr Gallagher sez 'is favourite song's that one that guz, "The only way is up", an' I reckon he might on to summat.

> Ho Ho for the robbers
> The cops an' the robbers Ho Ho!

POINT OF VIEW

Old Mother 'ubbard's written again. She is daft:

Dearest Paris,

I hope you are feeling O.K. Thank you for your letter, I feel a lot happier when I hear from you. I am working on a visit but I think it would be easier to arrange an audience with the Queen herself. I hope you are keeping busy. I know I am.

I keep going to work and I went out with the girls last Saturday. We went to "Jumpin Jaks". I was quite pleased because, although I was the oldest, I was asked to dance about four times and one man escorted me to the bar and bought me a drink and he didn't look half bad. It made a change from bingo and the geriatrics I usually encounter on my evening excursions. Last Sunday felt like spring but the weather has gone freezing cold again, I can't wait to get in and put the kettle on, put the heating on and just relax in my dressing gown ready for the next day at work. I keep trying to do crosswords at night to activate my brain because stacking slippers all day isn't very taxing really.

I can't wait to see you. I expect you've read a lot more books now. Tell me more about your studies. I think we have to be subjected to a sniffer dog looking for substances and have our photos taken. You know what I'm like about dogs but I'm sure you're worth it.

Tell the officers you are expecting some trainers, your mam is getting some.

Please write back soon,
I love you and miss you.
God bless

Mammar Joe (OMH!)
xxxx

So it's official. Everyone in Notts is havin' a better time than me, even ma friggin' Mammar! I'm pleased she had a good night, although I'm slightly amazed, to be honest. Asked to dance? Escorted to the bar? Not sure where she's findin' these men, but they're clearly not the blokes I bump into on nights out. I don't like the thought of Old Mother 'ubbard dancin' wi' strangers. I know what men can be like. Maybe they're more respectful though coz she's older. An' coz she's a real woman.

I showed Mr Gallagher ma letter an' he asked me how old Mammar Joe is. When I told 'im she's fifty-two he went, "Fifty-two! When's she comin' to visit?" He's sixty-four. 'Is wife died ten years ago. I actually wun't mind Mr Gallagher as a step-grandad, but I reckon Mammar Joe's had enough trouble wi' men as it is. Uncle Andy an' Uncle Roger, for starters. I mean honestly, as if one alcoholic weren't enough. Then there's Bernard. 'Er other brother. Died in a car crash. It worra twenty-first birthday present. She's gorra picture of 'im standin' next to it, big smile an' hair all slicked back, car freshly polished. He looked so pleased with 'issen. Mammar Joe would never have a favourite brother or sister, but if she did I reckon it may well have bin 'im. She sez only the good get taken young, an' only the wicked grow old. "So that bastard'll probably live to be a 'undred." She only swears when she's talkin' about Aunty Ray's dad.

Mam an' Aunty Ray are half-sisters. Like me an' ma brother, Jordan. Except we share a dad. Aunty Ray still lives with 'er dad. Mammar Joe lives on a council estate. I wish I could buy 'er a nice house. Ya need to give 'em a suitable address before ya can even be considered for HDC, so she sez I can come an' live with 'er when I ger-rout. She likes lookin' after me. We always have a cuppa an' a cuddle. Mammar Joe loves bein' cosy. Bein' cosy an' biscuits.

I feel bad about upsettin' 'er coz I know how much she worries about me. She stays up all night when I go out. She just sits there rockin' backwards an' forwards on the futon, smokin' roll-ups. She loves watchin' old films on Channel 5. When Gaz said I cun' go to actin' lessons – ya can guess why – she signed the consent form an' took me anyway. She sez, "Yer alright wi' me, duck." She's never minded me dressin' up or owt. She sez, "I just want you, ya mother an' Aunty Ray to be alright. That's all I'm bothered about." I know what she means now.

BODYSWERVE

"If yer not back by seven on the dot, we'll find ya an' take ya back to prison. If ya tamper wi' the tag or the box in any way, we'll find ya an' take ya back to prison. If ya get in any trouble – if ya so much as get a warnin' from the police – we'll find out, find ya, an' take ya back to prison. So what are ya gonna do?" I sez, "I'm gonna be good as gold an' be back by seven every day." He sez, "Ya better be, if ya know what's good for ya." The tag's linked to a box they've attached to the wall by the front door at Mammar Joe's. Mam wanted to meet me at the prison gates, but I just wanted to be on ma own. Everyone had bin sayin', "Just think how good yer gonna feel" an' I did, but I were sad too coz I just wish it'd never happened in the first place.

I feel like everythin's changed while I've bin away. Everyone's obsessed wi' R 'n' B an' hip hop now. No one listens to trance any more.

Tell ya summat though, next door don't say nowt to me now they know I've bin inside. They don't dare! I'm queen o' this fuckin' council estate now. There's only one room at Mammar Joe's, wi' two wooden beds an' a set of drawers between 'em. Mammar's gorra bookshelf full of faded novels from the eighties on 'er side that Mam sez she should chuck coz she never reads 'em. One of 'em shows a woman on a pirate ship bein' kissed by a man wi' no top on. It's called *Seaswept Abandon*. Other titles include *Betray Not My Passion* an' *The Vixen's Revenge*, which does look quite good, actually. But why would Mammar Joe wanna read owt like that?

I don't think she's bothered about sex. Well, I know she had me mam an' Aunty Ray, but she's definitely not done owt like that since i've bin alive. I ask 'er why she don't get a fella sometimes an' she guz, "I can't be doin' with all that. I've got enough problems, duck." Poor old Mr Gallagher'll be disappointed! I reckon she likes a flirt when she guz down the Constitutional, though. Everyone knows 'er there coz she used to work behind the bar. She guz every Friday an' drinks lager. Mam sez that's common. She don't come round to Old Mother 'ubbard's very often coz she sez it's scruffy, an' she lives in a nice house wi' Bobby now. They're gerrin married.

I don't understand how Old Mother 'ubbard don't wake 'ersen up sometimes. I have to shout an' tell 'er to turn over every night! I can't relax hearin' 'er strugglin' to breathe like that, it sounds like she's gonna choke. People are so vulnerable when they're asleep, aren't they? It just makes ya realize how we're just bits of flesh really. Organized meat. I lie there an' think about 'er heart, an' how it's bin in 'er chest, beatin' continuously for over fifty years. That's longer than I've bin alive – longer than Mam's bin alive! An' how it won't pump for ever. It makes me dead sad coz I don't know what I'd do without' Mammar Joe. I don't even like thinkin' about it.

She got me a wardrobe from IKEA while I were away an' Aunty Ray gorrit all set up for me for when I come out. It takes up a bit of space but it's good coz I can fit everythin' in it. I've told 'er not to go through ma stuff any more though, coz she found some rude poems me an' Lady Die wrote an' guz, "Look, I've got summat to ask ya. Ya an't got that HIV, have ya?" I sez, "Don't go readin' ma stuff, that's our sense of humour." But she worries.

Mam sez that when she were little Mammar Joe used to wake 'er up an' take 'er out in the middle o' the night. Apparently ya could buy fags from machines in the street back then so she'd put Aunty Ray in the pram an' take 'em all to the phone box an' call Mammar Molly. Mammar Molly was ma great-grandma. She died when I were little. Mammar Joe would leave Aunty Ray in the pram outside, but Mam had to go in the booth with 'er an' she'd hear 'er tellin' Mammar Molly that she thought 'er heart was just gonna stop beatin'. It used to really upset me mam coz she thought Mammar Joe were gonna drop dead an' she'd just be left there.

Mam sez she should've bin in bed. She must've only bin about five or six if Aunty Ray was in a pram. But *she* used to take *me* out in the middle o' the night to wait for Gaz to come back from the pub to catch 'im with other women. I remember 'er doin' up the buttons on ma duffle coat one winter an' seein' the steam on ma breath. Mammar Joe's still got bad nerves, she's always sayin', "God, gimme *strength*!" or "I'm abaht ready for a Valium, I am."

Apparently it calms ya down. They were dead poor when she were growin' up. She's got about ten brothers an' sisters an' apparently Mammar Molly used to make angel cake an' cut it so thin "ya could read the paper through it". Mammar Joe asked where 'er pet rabbit was once an' they were eatin' it. They'd put it in a stew.

She did it again yesterday. She sez, "I've found summat." I could hear she were worried. "Is it heroin? I know it's drugs." She'd found ma hash. Silly old Mammar! I sez, "It's like cannabis, ya must have heard o' that. That not hurt nowt." She guz, "Hash! What does that do?" I sez, "It calms ya down." Well, she seemed to like the sound o' that. She guz, "Ya don't inject it, do ya?" I explain that ya just sprinkle it wi' some tobacco an' smoke it. She guz, "Like a roll-up?" So I sez, "Yeah. Ya can try some if ya like." She guz, "Ner! I'm not tekkin' bleddy drugs!" I sez, "It's probably better than that baccy substitute Aunty Ray got ya from Holland & Barrett."

She's smoked since she was twelve. Uncle Andy sez when she were fourteen she took a pin an' stuck it through the nub of a roll-up someone had thrown away to get the final puffs out of it. She liked the Beatles back then. I sez, "Mammar, you've had stronger cups of tea." An' I bet she has, coz she's a right tea-belly, Old Mother 'ubbard. I make a roll-up an' sprinkle a bit in. Literally the lightest dustin' you've ever seen. I've had thicker layers of pepper on scrambled eggs.

I go first, then hand it to 'er. She guz, "Are ya sure this in't that heroin? Coz they smoke that, don't they?" I sez, "Maybe they do, but I'm hardly gonna gi' ma Mammar heroin am I?" So she takes it off me an' holds it up to the light to inspect it. I'm half expectin' 'er to jump up an' flush it down the loo, but then she puts it up to 'er lips an' takes a lil' puff. She holds it in for a second an' then breathes out. "Oh dear," she guz. "I feel a bit *funny*." Obviously I've burst out laughin' at this point. She hands it back to me an' sez, "Go on, that's the end of it now. Just promise me you'll never take that heroin. It ruins people's lives." I promise 'er, although I've always wanted to try it. Coz she's right, people do ruin their lives for it. It must be brilliant.

ONE MORE TIME

Guess who's gone an' got their curfew extended? I'm good, aren't I? Told probation I wanna go back to work at Robin Hood Resorts, so they phoned Stella up. She told 'em I'm a "valued employee" an' can't wait to have me back. An' they know I've bin goin' to college coz they spoke to ma tutor. I sez, "Look, I just wanna get ma life back on track. I've got college in the day, an' I'd really appreciate any help ya can offer." You'd think they'd be pleased. I know a lad who were let out on a Friday an' were back in again by Monday. They din't even put anyone in 'is cell. Forty-eight hours. They may as well have left 'is sheets on. This woman at probation seemed impressed wi' me though, so she went off an' made 'er calls, an' they've done it! They've actually agreed to it. So I don't have to come back till nine now. The shift's usually six till nine, but Stella's lettin' me do five till eight, so I've got time to get the bus back. Nine o'clock! That's not bad, is it? They don't do that for everyone, ya know.

But I'm makin' nowt compared to Asha. She's actually becomin' a woman now, she's growin' 'er hair an' everythin'. I sez, "How come you've got so much friggin' money these days? New shoes, new clothes, taxis everywhere." An' they might look it, but I bet those hair extensions weren't cheap – an' she's never done a day's work in 'er life. Sez she advertises in the back o' this car magazine called *Exchange & Mart* as a "transsexual escort". She charges a hundred pounds an hour! She's got some cheek. She's already given it away to half of Notts, but I guess I'm no one to judge. That's a lot though, innit? More than I make all week at Robin Hood Resorts! So I'm gonna advertise in there too. If she can do it, so can I. I thought it were illegal, but ya just say ya offer "full massage services". People know what ya mean. An' I'm better-lookin' than 'er, so I'm gonna be loaded soon!

I still go an' see Peter – he used to send me money when I were "away", as Mammar Joe calls it. It's a funny one, coz Mam'd go mad if she knew about Peter, but he's not just a dirty old man, he actually cares about me. It's wrong what he does, though. He sez I can move in with 'im when ma tag comes off, but I wanna get ma own place in town. I love Mammar Joe, but I hate 'ucknall. But I've gorra do it properly this time. No more gerrin into trouble. It's time to grow up.

I hate bein' stuck indoors at the weekends. It's alright in the week coz I'm at college all day an' work all evenin', so I'm ready to come home by the time it gets to nine. But it's 'orrible on Sat'day nights, knowin' they're all out havin' fun. I'm allowed out at seven in the mornin', so I could go an' join 'em if I really wanted, coz they'd still be out partyin', but it's not the same, is it? Mind you, I'd look better than everyone else. The most excitement I get these days is racing back to make sure I don't miss ma curfew. I sit on the bench on Titchfield Park an' wait for the seconds on ma watch to hit eight fifty-five, then

I raz it! Through the graveyard, over the wall, across the road, round the corner, down the jitty an' up the cul-de-sac. I always make it! I like the danger. I get an adrenaline rush from it. Like when I used to run down stairs at Gaz's, before the bell struck five.

I'm not allowed to get this tag wet so Mammar Joe wraps it in cling film when I have a bath an' I have to leave ma leg raised out the water. She sez people use too much water these days. They only had a bath once a week when she were young, an' a flannel wash the rest o' the time. She still does it, she calls it 'er "ablutions". Silly old Mammar. I sez, "Well, thank God times change coz they'd have sent me down the pit an' died of polio by now or summat." To be fair, I do use a lotta water. I don't think she really minds, though.

There's only one good thing about this estate an' that's Mammar Joe's garden. We really struck lucky with it. It's a weird shape coz of how the road loops round an' meets the car park. Basically, she's got all the space that was left over after all the other gardens were marked out. An' it's private too. One end's all overgrown grass, with a rhubarb patch an' some strawberries an' that. I made a den underneath an elderberry bush once out of some MDF an' an old cardboard box. Mammar Joe let me take a pillow an' a blanket an' stay out there in the summer. I'd sit there with a book an' a torch an' I loved it coz it was totally hidden. I think she stayed up watchin' me till the sun come up.

But the best bit's the secret garden. We cun' even get into it at first. It was full o' brambles when the council gave 'er this place, but we cut it down an' made a path-way into the wood. She's got an apple tree an' five cherry trees. There's more trees next door so it's dark an' cool in summer. I've gorra tree house up the tallest. I can see into the livin' room from it. We're the upstairs flat. The livin' room's at the back. Mammar Joe pops 'er 'ead out an' shouts, "Ey up", when I'm in it, although I know she can't see me. She's as blind as a bat. The only thing she don't seem to have any trouble seein' is 'er bingo card. We have fruit crumble in the summer. It's dead easy to make. I like blackberry. Mammar Joe likes apple though. We don't get many cherries coz the birds always get there first. Rhubarb's ma favourite though, I peel it an' have it wi' sugar. I'd never buy it from the supermarket, coz I know how good it is fresh. Makes ya wonder how better everythin' else would taste fresh. I'll miss that garden.

FEEL GOOD INC.

We used to empty all the water out the bogs when I were in prison. Ya have to pump it out wi' the toilet brush. Me an' the lad on ma left had adjacent toilets, so if we emptied 'em at the same time, we could talk through the pipe. It stank at first – oh, it were 'orrible! – but it cleared after a bit. An' it gets even better. Coz if the lad above ya emptied 'is, all three of ya could talk. Ya could even talk to the lad above ya neighbour, an' the lad above 'im, an' 'is neighbour, too – although the higher up ya went, the harder it was to hear 'em. Six cells share one pipe before it guz to the main waste pipe. An' coz a lot of 'em shared a cell it meant that I had about ten people I could talk to at any given time. Well, in theory. It all depended on whether they felt like talkin' when you did, but some nights we'd all stay up chattin' for hours.

They all liked me in the end coz I used to sing an' read 'em rude poems. If ya can entertain people in prison, yer on to a winner. It were hard to know how many people were listenin' sometimes so ya had to be careful what ya said, an' there were other problems too. Like, ya could only talk to the lad two cells above ya if the lad in between agreed to empty 'is bog too. An' if ya were talkin' to yer neighbour an' someone else took a shit an' flushed it, it was fuckin' disgustin'. We had some proper

210

laughs, though. We'd talk about our lives on the outside, an' what we were gonna do when we got out. An' when ya got sick of 'talkin', ya just flushed it.

That were the first time I'd ever really spoken to straight lads without there bein' girls there. No one would talk to me when we did sports at school. But I've gorra mate who's straight now. I met 'im at Robin Hood Resorts. Asha reckons he's gay coz he don't mind hangin' out with us, but he sez he'd just tell people if we were coz he's not bothered about owt like that. I just feel like ya have to accept people at face value coz ya can't just tell someone who they are, can ya? But she's convinced. I reckon she just can't stand the fact he don't fancy 'er. I think she's a bit threatened by 'im, to be honest. He's a Muslim. I know. Ya cun' make it up, could ya?

He's from Saudi Arabia. 'Is name's Louai – it's pronounced "Loo-eye", apparently, but we just call 'im Louis. He's got long hair an' looks like the boy from that Cheltenham an' Gloucester advert who finds a pearl in the sea. He sounds American coz he sez he learned English at an international school, an' by watchin' *Friends*. I think that's dead bad. It's English, for God's sake. They should teach people how to speak it how we speak it. Well, maybe not how *we* speak it – but how like posh people speak it. Like how Joan Collins talks.

I've got ma own place in Sherwood now. Uncle John sez I'm doin' alright for mysen coz he din't have laminate floors when he were ma age. He liked ma stereo an' all. I've gorrit set up dead nice, an' I keep it dead clean. I love havin' ma own place, although I'm worried I'm gonna trip up while I'm hooverin' or summat an' no one'll be there to phone an ambulance. I thought about Max the night I moved in. I never heard from 'im after that first letter. I guess it's just never gonna be what I wanted it to be, is it? But I still love 'im. Which makes me sad, in some ways, but happy in others, coz I know it were love now. I wun't still have these feelin's after everythin' that's happened if it din't mean owt. It did mean summat, to me.

Louis lives in Sherwood round the corner from ma new place so we ended up catchin' the same bus last week. Awkward, innit, when ya end up sittin' near someone ya sorta know, coz then ya have to make small talk with 'em. He guz, "Have you got any plans for the weekend?" I sez, "I'm havin' a party, d'ya wanna come?" I weren't actually gonna have a party till I said that, but I thought, Why not, eh? Now, I din't know nowt about this Louis, an' he din't know nowt about me, so I sez, "Look, Louis, I should probably warn ya I hang about with a pretty wild crowd." But he just laughed an' sez he weren't bothered. By the time he come round I'd gorra full face of makeup on an' Lady Die had laid the bathroom mirror on the bed an' was linin' up some coke. Asha were kneeling beside 'er patiently, in not much more than a bra. I sez, "Hiya Lou, d'ya wanna drink? I hope yer not shy. I forgot to tell ya, I'm a transsexual." Then I pointed to Die an' sez, "An' she's a drug addict." Asha lifts 'er head up from the mirror an' shouts, "*An'* a prostitute!"

Well, this Louis were fresh off the boat, so he'd never

done drugs or owt like that. He sez they don't even have gay people in Saudi Arabia, an' it's illegal to drink. 'Is mam weren't allowed to drive out there an' she lived there for twenty years. She's English, but she married an Arab an' moved there in the eighties, but they've fallen out now, so she's come back. I sez, "How could she leave Britain in the eighties? There was Boy George an' everythin'. But she sez there were Thatcher too." He's gorra younger brother here, but the youngest two are still with 'is dad. I feel a bit bad really coz ya know how they say someone's "got in with a bad crowd"? Well, this Louis's dead nice, an' we're just about the worst crowd in Notts.

OOPS (OH MY)

I've bin burgled. They broke in through the sash window while I were out. It's ma own fault. The police come round an' said I should tell ma landlord I need proper locks coz I'd bin securin' the window with a nail – which I'd quite liked, coz it were like bein' in Olden Times – but it's a bit late now, innit? I feel violated. It's dead weird knowin' people have bin through all yer stuff. It just don't feel like ma home any more. An' I dunno why, but I can't help thinkin' that Asha's got summat to do with it. I try not to be paranoid these days, but she knew I had ma computer an' stereo in there. It's got all ma pictures on it, an' ma personal details. Ma CV. Mammar Joe sez it's a shame no one ever comes to burgle 'er, "Coz they might take pity on me an' leave summat." She was tryna cheer me up, but I know she's dead worried about me really. She keeps beggin' me to move back in with 'er.

I'm not goin back to 'ucknall though, so I phoned Louis. He turned up five minutes later, bless 'im. I told 'im I din't feel safe so he sez, "You can stay at ours if you like. I'm sure my mom won't mind." 'Is mam's a bit older than mine, say mid forties, but she looks dead good. She's quite middle class an' has loadsa books. She's an English teacher, so I tell 'er I'm studyin' English literature at college. She sez, "Oh yes, stay with us. I wouldn't

feel safe sleeping somewhere by myself if I'd been burgled!" an' made me up a spare bed in the attic room.

She's got piles an' piles o' books in the back room an'
took me to rummage round for Christopher Marlowe
with 'er. She's dead passionate about books, ya know
how English teachers are. She sez, "Would you like a
glass of wine?" Well, I've never drunk red, but ma nerves
were bad after bein' burgled so I sez, "Oh, thank you
very much." She sez, "What do you like to read?" so I
tell 'er I like *Great Expectations*, an' *Macbeth*. She asked me
worra liked about *Great Expectations*, an' I sez, "Miss
Havisham." So then she's like, "What about *Macbeth*?"
So I guz, "I like Lady Macbeth, coz when Macbeth
breaks 'is promise she said she'd dash a baby's brains out
if she'd promised to. Coz a lotta men lie an' I think
people should keep their promises." She sez I could stay
as long as I like.

I might just do that. After she'd gone to bed, Louis
asked me if I wanted to watch a film. Sez he'd got some
chocolate, did I want some? But he din't wanna watch an
action film or owt like that. He guz, "Have ya heard of
Almodóvar? He's a Spanish director." Sez he got into
'im when he were doin' 'is gap year in Spain. I thought,
Ooh, a gap year sounds posh. So we watched it in Spanish, an' we weren't tired after it finished so we watched
V for Vendetta straight after. 'Is house is dead cosy. We
sat on the sofa an' when 'is foot touched ma leg he din't
pull away. There were nowt sexual about it. I know when
guys are bein' like that. He's just comfortable round me.
It were like sittin' wi' Mammar Joe.

I cun' believe it. I just sat there thinkin', 'Is foot's touchin' me an' he's not even bothered! He's not treatin' me like I'm a leper. No one would even sit next to me at school, let alone touch me. The only time lads ever touched me at school was to hit me. Same wi' Gaz, come to think of it. Even Stephen Gatten – ma only boy mate – wun't walk home wi' me coz he din't wanna be seen wi' me. An' he turned out to be gay 'issen! But this Louis treats me like I'm a normal person. I spoke to 'is lil' brother before he went to bed, an' he was fine wi' me too. I've never known owt like it.

I sez, "Aren't ya bothered about the way I am? Coz they murder people for bein' gay in Saudi Arabia, don't they?" But he sez that, coz officially there's no gay people in Saudi, in some ways people aren't as paranoid about bein' seen as gay. Men can walk around holdin' hands an' no one bats an eyelid. Like how girls can link arms over here. I sez, "Well, why don't *you* have a problem with it?" But he sez 'is mam's Western so he's a bit more open-minded. Sez there are gay people in Saudi, but they just have to keep quiet about it. Like they did here not that long ago. But I start wonderin' what people like me do out there? Coz it's one thing hidin' the fact yer gay, but what about transsexuals? Louis sez he's never met any, but they must be out there, an it must be awful for 'em. So that's how I've ended up livin' in a house of Muslims, who've made me feel more welcome than ma own family.

I went back to 'ucknall the other day to see Mammar Joe an' bumped into Mam outside the Co-op. I sez, "Shall I come back wi' ya for a cup of tea?" But she sez,

"I don't think now's the best time, really." I were wearin' mascara an' she said Bobby's daughter was home an' she din't want me confusin' 'er. I sez, "What ya worried about, that she might grow up an' wear mascara?" Well, fuck 'er. What sorta mam makes ya feel unwelcome? Mammar Joe would never treat me like that.

She sez how I live ma life's up to me now, but that don't mean she has to have me rubbin' it in 'er face. "How can ya turn around an' say ya wanna be a woman? Ya said ya were gay." But I only said that coz everyone told me it wasn't possible to become a woman. An' I believed 'em, till I saw Nadia on *Big Brother*. I were in prison an' they were takin' the piss out of 'er on *Bo' Selecta!* He dressed up as 'er. He had a short skirt on an' a pair of rubber bollocks that kept fallin' down every time he crossed 'is legs. But inside the house, everyone was alright wi' 'er. An' it blew ma mind, coz you'd have bin more likely to see an alien walkin' down 'ucknall High Street than meet a transsexual. But she showed me it's possible. That I could still have mates, an' go to college. Walk into shops. Talk to people. Be a normal person. That there were at least some people who'd treat me wi' respect.

Mam sez it's a phase. Yeah, an eighteen-year phase, Lisa. I'll show ya worra phase is. I'll show everyone. They might not know who I am, but I do.

READY OR NOT

I took the biggest breath I could manage, ma thoracic cavity expandin' as air rushed down ma trachea an' into ma lungs. Or, to be more precise, the primary bronchi, which branch out to yer secondary an' tertiary bronchi, an', eventually, the lobules. Makes me laugh, that word. Well, each o' these lobules consists of a bronchiole, which branches out into alveolar ducts. Ducts lead to a group of alveolar sacs – little round pockets of tissue – an' that, ladies an' gentlemen, is where yer gas exchange occurs. Yer body's amazin' inside. All o' the lower respiratory tract is lined wi' respiratory epithelium, which is carpeted wi' cilia, tiny hair-like structures that help waft dirt away wi' the mucus produced by goblet cells. Alveoli are made up of squamous epithelial cells. They have extremely thin walls that enable easy gas exchange.

I know all this coz I'm doin' human biology at college. They had a spirometer today an' it turns out I've got the largest vital lung capacity in the class. I know it's a ridiculous thing to gerra big 'ead about, but for someone who hates sport an' has smoked Superking Blacks for five years, I'm not gonna lie, I'm chuffed. Imagine how healthy I'd be if I looked after mysen.

I love bein' at college. I'm so grateful that I've gorra

second chance. I copy ma notes up dead neat when I get home. I'm doin' English an' psychology, coz I wanna understand people. But the notes from biology look dead cool coz I do little drawin's of mitochondria an' stuff, an' colour 'em in an' that. It makes me proud lookin' at worrav done. We got some sheep's lungs once an' inflated 'em. It were dead weird. There's this big muscle at the bottom of yer thoracic cavity an' when it contracts it drags the lungs down, so air gets sucked in to fill in the vacuum. It's dead interestin'.

But I really, really, really wish I din't know so much about lungs right now. Coz I'm sittin' by a hospital bed wi' Mammar Joe in it, listenin' to 'er strugglin' to breathe. An' all I can think about is those sheep's lungs, an' what Mammar Joe's must look like.

Aunty Ray called me on Friday night. I were at home watchin' TV an' she guz, "Can ya get to the hospital as quick as ya can?" So I ordered a taxi. She was stood waitin' for me outside A&E. Mammar Joe had asked 'er to come round coz she were feelin' really poorly. Sez she cun' breathe. She'd left bleach down the bog an' thought it were just that, but Aunty Ray sez as soon as she laid 'er eyes on 'er she knew it was summat serious. When I went in, she was sat on a stretcher wearin' a gown an' an oxygen mask. Ya could see 'er dandruff in the bright lights. She's got lovely dark hair, Old Mother 'ubbard. Same colour as mine. She's only gorra few greys, which in't bad for a Mammar, is it?

She were diagnosed with emphysema a few years ago, but she carried on smokin'. Aunty Ray's tried everythin' to get 'er to quit, but ya can't force someone, can ya? We all begged 'er. But she wun't listen. Aunty Ray even threatened to stop visitin' 'er if she din't stop, coz she sez she wants 'er to live a long life an' be around to see 'er have kids one day. She used to hide Mammar Joe's fags when she were little, coz even then they knew it were bad for ya. An' yet here I am, standin' outside A&E, smokin' like there's no tomorrow. I sez, "I'm sorry Aunty Ray, but I need this."

She sez, "She'll get through this, ya know? Mammar Joe's a fighter." But she's lookin' up at the stars, like she's not really talkin' to me, like she's sayin' it to the universe. An' I'm thinkin', No, she's not. I love Mammar Joe to bits, but out of everyone I know she's the person most likely to just drop down dead at any minute. I call Mam up afterwards an' she sez exactly the same thing. "But don't say that to Aunty Ray."

THE TIME IS NOW

The nurse is askin' me what ma relationship with 'er is. So I tell 'er she's ma mammar an' she guz, "Ah, OK", an' walks off. Well, I'm not havin' that, am I, so I follow 'er to the desk an' say, "What's goin' on? Have ya got 'er results?" But she sez she can't tell me coz I'm not "immediate family". I'm like, "Are ya kiddin' me? She brought me up, for God's sake. Why d'ya think I'm here? D'ya think I'm sat there sobbin' coz I'm a distant relative?" They told us to go home last night, but I've bin here all morning. Aunty Ray stayed all night. She's gone home to shower now. I shoulda just said, "She's me mam." Coz honestly, I wish she was. I sez, "So you're tellin' me you've got information in yer hand an' ya won't share it wi' me coz she din't give birth to me? An' yer gonna make me wait till me mam gets here, like she's more important than me?"

Mam don't even visit 'er! I live with 'er, for fuck's sake! But I'm not allowed to know how ill she is? I'm fumin'. I run out an' call me mam, tell 'er to get here as soon as possible. But as I'm about to go back in an' demand to speak to someone higher up, Aunty Ray arrives. I don't wanna be anywhere near that nurse now, so I just go an' sit wi' Mammar Joe while Aunty Ray talks to 'er. I'm lookin' over at 'em an' thinkin' how good Aunty Ray is at calmin' things down. But then she bursts out cryin', an' I know. I just *know*.

The doctor comes over an' pulls the curtain round Mammar Joe's bed, an' takes us to one side. Lowers 'is voice an' sez they've looked at the X-rays an' she's got lung cancer, an' it's spread all through 'er body. Sez there's nowt they can do to help 'er. Aunty Ray asks 'im how long she's got an' he guz, "No one can say for sure in these situations, but you'd better prepare yourself for the worst. I'm afraid we're looking at a couple of days, if that."

He pulls back the curtain an' taps Mammar Joe on the shoulder. "Josephine, can you hear me?" She makes a sorta grunt an' guz, "Yeah." I can't stand to hear 'er like this.

"Are you in pain?"

"Yeah."

"We're going to give you something for that. Do you want to hear your test results?"

"No."

"You're very ill though, Josephine. You know that, don't you?"

"Yeah."

Then he comes back an' pulls the curtain round again. Sez he don't see any point tellin' 'er exactly what's happenin'. "I think she knows," he sez. "People tend to know."

The ward overlooks the grounds. Ya can see the trees swayin' in the wind. It's summer, technically, but there's still a bit o' spring in the air. The whole world seems to be burstin' wi' life, just to rub our noses in it. There's no privacy. Ya can hear the people talkin' to their visitors.

An old woman on the other side o' the ward opened 'er bowels earlier. I've never smelled owt like it in ma entire life. It was like death. The nurse asked Mammar Joe if she wanted some tea, an' I burst into tears coz I thought this could be 'er last cup of tea. An' it was. She took two sips with a straw then slipped out of consciousness. I just sat starin' at it, thinkin', She's never gonna finish that. She's never gonna finish a cup of tea again.

At about one a.m., Aunty Ray tells me mam to go home an' get some rest. We promise to call 'er if Mammar Joe gets worse. I mean, it's a bit of a risk, innit, but I don't think any of us can actually believe she's gonna die. Coz it's all so sudden. How can ya have lung cancer an' not know it? People know when they've got cancer, these days. Who the hell just turns up to A&E dyin' o' cancer? Cancer's not menna be an emergency. It don't make no sense.

There's nowhere to sleep, but the nurse said we could use the visitors' room at the end o' the corridor if we wanted. It's just a little room with a sofa in it, an' ya can't really make it dark coz it's attached to the corridor by a frosted glass wall, but I managed to get half an hour or so in there earlier, so I've told Aunty Ray to go an' have a lie-down for a bit. She was up all night. I'm used to stayin' up on Sat'day nights anyway. Wonder what them lot are doin'.

They turn the lights off on the ward at night, but there's light comin' in from the windows above the doors. They're covered in a blue plastic film so everythin' looks like the end of *Titanic* when Jack's dyin'. Mammar Joe looks like death. I'd always thought that gerrin ya heart broken were just a turn of phrase, but I could actually feel it happenin' to me when the doctor said she was dyin'. It was like a chemical reaction had bin set off in ma heart, an' I could feel it spreadin' into the rest of ma body, like poison. I din't know it were even possible to feel like this. It's amazin', really. Just think, all this time ma body's had the power to make me feel this bad. Funny, innit? The chemicals must've have bin sittin' there all that time, in ma brain, waitin' for the trigger.

Grief's like one o' them things ya can read about or see on the telly, but ya just can't understand till you've bin through it. Like puberty, or fallin' in love. Ya think ya know what it's all about, but until it happens to you, really it's just words. Like grief. An' heartbreak. But they're not just words to me now. I know what they describe. This.

But as I'm sat thinkin', Mammar Joe's head jolts like she's tryna cough. I jump up an' try to put ma hand behind 'er 'ead, but then blood starts spurtin' out 'er mouth. I don't know what to do – I don't wanna shout coz everyone's asleep, but she's chokin'. So I have to. I call the nurse as quietly as I can an' try an' sit 'er up, but she can't hear. I'm thinkin', Oh God, she can't breathe. The blood looks purple in the light, an' I can't stand to see Mammar Joe like this so I run to the desk an' beg 'em to come an' help. They come straight over an' I just stand there while they prop 'er up an' open up 'er airways. I don't know what to do wi' mysen, so I go an' wake up Aunty Ray.

They got 'er breathin' again, but they say she's goin' downhill an' we should call anyone she'd want to be with 'er. Sez they'll find us a private room. Aunty Ray sez I've gorra try an' get some sleep till they're ready to move 'er, but I just keep driftin' in an' out of nightmares.

The doctor sez we should keep talkin' to 'er coz yer hearin's the last thing to go. I think he said it to comfort us, but I find that quite terrifyin' actually. Coz it must be so frightenin', not bein' able to speak. An' lonely. To be trapped an' in pain, an' know yer body is dyin'. Mammar Joe's biggest fear is havin' an operation an' the anaesthetic wearin' off enough for 'er to feel pain, but not bein' able to scream. She saw a documentary about it once on Channel 5. An' I agree, it sounds unbearable. So I'm wonderin' if that's how she feels now. Scared. Powerless. Voiceless.

I never felt like I could speak up at Gaz's. I remember one Bonfire Night when I were little – I must've bin about seven or eight – an' Aunty Ray dropped me off at Mammar Rita's. It were Mammar Rita's birthday so there were fireworks an' a barbeque, an' all ma dad's side o' the family were there. Aunty Ray had 'er car window down an' Gaz asked 'er if she wanted to join us, but she said, "No thanks, I'm a vegetarian." After she left, he started mouthin' off about how she worra stuck up cow an' how 'er an' me mam are "cut from the same fuckin' cloth". Then he called me mam a tosser. I had to listen to 'im slag 'em off in front of all ma aunties an' cousins. I really wanted to speak up, coz Aunty Ray an't gorra nasty bone in 'er body, but I were too scared. I guess everyone else was too, coz no one said a word. I just sat an' kept ma mouth shut.

What would Mammar Joe say if she could speak?

We sit for hours, till the sun comes up, just holdin' Mammar's hands. An' ya know how sometimes a song'll come into yer head that reminds ya of whatever it is yer doin'? Well, all I can hear is Moloko. "The Time Is Now". *You're my last breath, You're a breath of fresh air to me.* She looks so helpless. She's only fifty-two. That's no age to die, is it? 'Er hands are covered wi' purple veins, like the witch in *Snow White*. But they still look lovely to me, small an' soft an' feminine. In fact, everythin' about Mammar Joe is small, soft an' feminine, which is weird coz I've never even thought about it before but it's like I'm seein' 'er wi' fresh eyes. Mam's veins are startin' to show now. I'd never noticed that before either, but they look older next to Aunty Ray's. Hers have a bit of wear an' tear too, but not as much as me mam's. Mine are white an' smooth.

Then me mam looks up an' sez, "I think we should get 'er a priest." Old Mother 'ubbard never guz to church, but she wears St Christopher round 'er neck, so we reckon it's worth a try. Mam guz an' speaks to the nurse, an' ten minutes later a man wearin' black turns up hol-din' a bible. He sez, "So you're her daughters, then", an' we're all so shocked that no one contradicts 'im, but I like it. Then he starts talkin' about God an' Heaven, an' it all sounds so strange, but it's also kinda comfortin'. After he leaves, Mam sez, "I'm sorry, Mam. I've bin angry wi' ya all these years, but none o' that matters now. I know I've not always bin the best daughter, but ya know I love ya, don't ya?" I don't know what exactly Mam is menna be angry wi' Mammar Joe for, but I've got nothin' to forgive, so I just tell 'er I love 'er. Aunty Ray's talkin' about all the nice things they've done, all their happy memories. Then me mam sez, "Ya can go, ya know, Mam."

Then all of a sudden, Mammar Joe's fingertips turn cold. I face me mam an' she's starin' back at me with a look of horror – like she's just seen Death 'issen. An' we know. This is it. It starts at the tips, an' spreads down 'er fingers, like a wave. I can actually feel the flesh turnin' cold as the blood retreats an' 'er life slips away. I move ma hands up to 'er wrists, but then they go cold too, as it sweeps up 'er arm. She's makin' these awful noises. Aunty Ray sez it's a death rattle. They're gerrin further an' further apart, an' more an' more upsettin'. Each time I think, This one's gotta be the last, but then there's another. An' I suddenly get this overwhelmin' urge to shout for the doctors, coz she don't wanna die! She wants to live! She's tryin' 'er best to breathe, for God's sake! We can't just let 'er die. She must be scared, coz I would be! I'd be terrified. An' I'd want people to come an' save me.

Coz until she's actually dead, there's still hope, in't there? An' I'm wonderin' why the fuck we just accepted what the doctors told us? Coz they could be doin' more for 'er, I know they could. I bet she'd be gerrin better care than this if she were the Queen! They don't die at fifty-two, do they, the Royal Family. So why can't they give 'er what they'd give them? There must be more they can do!

But then she dies. One minute she's there – the next she's not.

The thing that gets me the most is knowin' that every second for the rest of ma life is gonna take me further away from this moment, from 'er bein' alive. That I'll grow older, an' I'll change, an' I'll always be travellin' away from now. It's like bein' on a spaceship an' watchin' the earth get further away, knowin' you'll never be able to go home again.

How could she have not known she were dyin'? Mam sez, "I don't remember a single day where she said she felt well 'er whole life." An' it's true, Mammar Joe was a bit of a hypochondriac. I'd say, "How's it goin', Old Mother 'ubbard?" An' she'd go, "I'm not feelin' too well, duck. But I'll be rate after a cuppa tea." But when she did actually have summat seriously wrong with 'er, she just ignored it. It's absolutely ridiculous. There's no way she cun' have known she was dyin'. Aunty Ray sez she must have done, deep down, but just din't wanna face it.

I've taken most of 'er stuff. The council said we had two weeks to clear 'er flat out, so Mam ordered a skip. She were walkin' around goin', "Just throw that, no one's gonna use that." She wants to throw everythin', but Aunty Ray's followin' 'er round sayin', "No, that can go ter charity that can, Lisa." I found a T-shirt that sez Mencap on it, an' it made me think about the summer she volunteered for 'em while Mam was abroad, coz I used to go down Nottingham with 'er an' I made loadsa friends. We did loadsa stuff together, me an' Old Mother 'ubbard.

I keep hearin' 'er sayin', "Put that down, I'm savin' that!" like she's right next to me, coz she worra right hoarder. I think it's coz she were dead poor growin' up.

She'd absolutely hate the thought of all this bein' thrown in the skip. I snatch a glass casserole dish that me mam's about to toss in a bin liner an' she guz, "Ya can't keep that, it's filthy. You'll get a disease." I sez, "She din't die from a disease, she died from fags. Which I notice you're still smokin'!" I've not bin able to have one since Mammar Joe died. They're absolutely disgustin'.

She sez, "Yer eighteen years old, ya can't take everythin'."

I sez, "I can do worra want. You don't have to take it, but ya can't stop me!"

She sez, "We're all hurtin', Byron. She were ma mam, ya know."

I sez, "I know exactly who she was, an' she knew exactly who I am too – that's why she din't call me Byron. She called me what *I* wanna be called. Coz she's bin more of a mam to me than you have." An' I can feel what's comin' next, but it's like drivin' a car ya know's about to crash, but ya just can't take yer foot off the accelerator – "I wish it had bin *you*! I wish *you'd* fuckin' died, not 'er!" An' I'm thinkin', Fuck off! Fuck off! Fuck off! I know I'm wrong for sayin' it, I know I've gone too far. But I just wish Mammar Joe was still here. All the 'orrible people in the world, an' the universe leaves 'em an' comes an' takes 'er. All the murderers, an' the war criminals, they just live on an' on, don't they?

An' then – just as I'm thinkin' about 'orrible old bastards that refuse to die – Gaz turns up. I've not seen 'im for about a year. An' would ya believe, he's more concerned about me mam than me? Ma fuckin' dad! Apparently. An' he's still in love with 'er, after all these years. He loves 'er more than me! He's literally stood there comfortin' 'er, an' ignorin' me. An' I don't care what anyone sez, I *do* wish it had bin 'im. I really do. How on earth is he still walkin' about while Mammar Joe is dead?

I hate 'im. I do. So why do I wish he'd put 'is arms around me an' tell me he loves me, that everythin's gonna be alright? But he won't. An' it's not. I feel ashamed for even thinkin' it.

He were sat in the livin' room an' I accidentally knocked 'is foot when I come back from the loo. I sez, "Sorry", an' he guz, "What for? The past four years?" It took me a moment to process it at first. *Sorry for the past four years?* An' then I realize, he thinks I've bin misbehavin' all this time! That I'm a naughty teenager. That I've done summat wrong. To *him*. That I need to apologize for. Right now, the day after Mammar Joe's died. He din't even know 'er that well. I'm mournin' for someone who's bin more of a parent to me than both o' them put together, an' he's just sittin' there makin' snide comments. I fuckin' hate 'im.

But I've already said enough today. Aunty Ray always sez, "If ya an't got owt nice to say, don't say owt at all." An' it's true, innit, coz there's no need to be nasty most the time. She always taught me it's important to be kind to people, even if they're not kind to you. It's so hard sometimes though. I look at Gaz an' me mam, an' can't believe I've bin left here wi' these selfish fuckin' idiots. I walk out. Looks like I'm gonna have to look after mysen from now on.

PUT YOUR HANDS UP
FOR DETROIT

I saw Lady Die in town. She guz out dressed up in the day now. She were wearin' jeans, big hoop earrin's an' a Von Dutch cap. I sez, "Oi, Die, not like you to wear clothes!" She come over an' said she's sorry to hear about Mammar Joe, an' sparked up a fag. We were stood at the Left Lion. She said, "D'ya want one?" so I just looked at 'er like, do me a favour, babe. Mam sez it's scandalous they're even allowed to sell fags, that there's people who've got rich sellin' things they know are bad for ya. I mean, it's not as if anyone's forcin' people to smoke, but she's right. It's wrong. They used to tell people cigarettes were good for 'em.

People are starin' at Lady Die as she's sparkin' up this fag though, an' then these two lads shout, "Gizza light, mate!" She just pretends she can't 'ear 'em. An' I'm thinkin', I can't do this. I can't deal wi' this every day for the rest of ma life. Then one of 'em shouts, "Oi, nigger-bloke, what ya ignorin' me for?" so she turns round an' tells 'em to fuck off. Next thing I know they dash over an' knock 'er cap off. 'Er wig comes loose an' as she's tryna straighten up one thumps 'er in the back of 'er 'ead an' spits on 'er. Everyone's lookin'. I'm so shocked, I can't even think. Before I can even process what's just gone off, they shout, "Fuckin' battyman", an' run off. Die's shakin'.

I go, "Babe, are ya alright?" an' pick 'er cap up. She's stylin' it out, tryna pretend they've not upset 'er, but they have, I know they have. Coz I know how it feels. I go, "Come on, let's go to the police, I bet they're on CCTV", but she sez, "I can't be doin' with it", so I'm like, "Are ya sure? Coz ya pulled that fit policeman last time we went", an' then she's gorra smile on 'er face again, which makes me smile but inside I'm seethin' wi' them bastards. All this is menna stop when ya leave school an' Die's twenty now, for God's sake. An' it's just so unfair coz she wun't hurt a fly, Die. OK, she's one of Nottingham's most infamous slags, but she wun't ever be nasty to anyone. An' I'm gonna miss 'er like summat rotten if I leave Notts. She's the mint sauce to ma mushy peas.

But it made me think, I'm not gonna call 'er a black bitch again. Coz it's not the same when she calls me a white slag, is it? Coz OK, I can't dance, an' I've got no hips, but no one's actually tryna bully me for bein' white, are they? An' she's gerrin it coz she's a tranny *an'* coz she's black. The worst thing is though, they were black! So they should know what it feels like to be picked on for bein' different, an' yet they're doin' that to other people! It makes me sick.

I go, "You shun't let 'em get away wi' it, ya know? Ya don't deserve to be treated like that. No one does." An' I'm thinkin', The only way I can do it is if I can really pull it off. I've gorra look the part. I've gorra look like a girl. I go, "Die, d'ya think we'll ever be alright? If we have like loadsa surgery an' that? D'ya think people will ever accept us?" But she sez she don't know. "Can ya imagine if ya spent all that money an' people still din't see ya as a real woman? I think that'd be even more upsettin' than 'em not acceptin' us now."

She sez, "They've passed a law so ya can change yer passport now, ya know. Ya can say yer female now." Well, I din't know, but that makes me feel a bit better, coz it just shows ya, there must be other people out there like us. An' it's like the government's sayin' we're OK. That we're proper people. I'm gonna miss 'er so much. I don't think anyone's ever had as much fun as me an' Die.

I go, "Oi, Die, d'ya remember when we went to Newstead Abbey that time?" An' she guz, "Ah, that was fun that day!" Then she guz, "D'ya remember when we got kicked off the train at Loughborough coz we'd spent all our money on drugs, an' we had to go in Asda dressed like slags an' you said, 'Come on, there's no such thing as bad attention?' I sez, "How could I forget? Eh, d'ya remember that time yer blood sugar dropped at One Big Sunday in Leicester an' they let us go back stage an' meet Atomic Kitten, an' I thought you'd just done it for attention?" She guz, "Yeah, coz I nearly died."

I sez, "We have a laugh, don't we?" She guz, "Yeah, we do."

I don't even know if I should be applyin' to uni. Ya have to write to 'em an' ask for a place based on yer predicted grades, but how can I go to uni an' become a girl all in one month? It's too much! Louis's mam sez I should just do it, an' that if I don't I might never go an' it'd be a waste coz I've got potential. "Just think about all the hard work you've done to get here. Think about how proud your grandmother – your Mammar Joe – would be knowing that you're going to university." She's right, but Mammar Joe's not gonna know, is she? Why cun' she have died after I'd got ma A-level results? Why cun't she have seen that I'm good? At least she'd have known I were on the right path.

I sez, "Die, if I move dead faraway, will ya visit?"

She guz, "Just you try an' stop me."

"But what if the train's dead expensive?"

"I'll skank it."

WHAT YOU WAITING FOR?

I gorran A in English! I'm dead happy. B in human biology, C in psychology, an' a D in French. It's not gonna get me into Oxford any time soon, but I have bin offered a place at the University of Brighton. They wanted better grades, but ma tutor wrote to 'em an' told 'em I've had a tough few years but "would make a great addition to the university". She's bin really good to me, she has. Joanna Baker. So they're givin' me a chance! I've had another offer too, but I wanna go to Brighton. I cun' be arsed to research unis so I just picked a folder of prospectuses from the library at college an' applied to all of 'em. They're in alphabetical order. It was the one with all the Bs, so it were Bristol, Brighton or Birmingham. I've seen Brighton on the telly. Loadsa gay people live there, apparently. Peter sez the council's run by gays, so if I'm gonna be alright anywhere, it's there, innit?

I've bin doin' a lotta thinkin' since Mammar Joe died. About how short life is, an' all the things she coulda done but won't have the chance to now. An' I'm sick of hidin' who I am coz I'm scared what other people might think. Coz one day I'm gonna be dead, an' it'll be too late. An' I think Mammar Joe would want me to be happy. She was always sayin' how all she wanted was for me, me mam an' Aunty Ray to be alright. Well I know what I need to do to be happy now. I've always known, really.

Ma hair's growin'. I'll be able to put it in a pony tail soon. Mam sez I've got nice hair, not thin like hers. I got the bathroom mirror an' held it next to the wardrobe mirror so I could see ma face from every angle the other day, an' I actually think I can do it. I might just be alright. I'm lucky, really. I just don't wanna waste any more time. I'm so, so sick of lookin' at all the girls at college an' wishin' I could just be mysen. Coz it's never gonna go away, an' I don't just wanna be one o' them cross-dressers when I'm thirty. That's OK for some, but what's the point in wastin' any more years tryna be summat I'm not? I've wasted enough as it is.

I went to see me mam the other day an' told 'er I'm givin' all ma old clothes to Louis. Sez I'm gerrin laser hair removal on ma face. She sez, "Where ya gonna get the money for that?", but I think she knows, deep down. Who else has money for taxis all the time? She were sat at the bottom o' the stairs. I sez, "I don't know worram gonna do about this, though", an' put ma hand on ma chest. "Coz I'm never gonna be able to afford that." An' d'ya know what she sez to me? She sez, "Don't worry, we'll find a way." She's gonna help! She's finally startin' to gerrit. Or at least she sez she does.

Which is more than can be said for ma GP. Smanfa's boyfriend took me down an' they waited in the reception for me. I looked dead good, I wore ma Superdry hoodie wi' the long sleeves. I sez, "I wanna have a sex change," an' this doctor just looked at me gone out. I cun' believe

238

what she said next. "So, just to clarify, you want to become a man?" I burst out laughin'. I sez, "No, the other way round", so she sez she's gonna refer me to a psychiatrist. That's what ya have to do before they give ya owt. But I wanna start on the tablets as soon as possible.

I went to see Peter afterwards. He showed me a photo o' this new lad he's knockin' about with. Looks about seventeen. I can tell he's sweet on 'im, an' it made me realize that I were never really that special to 'im, was I? He'll just be on to the next, an' the next. I'm not sayin' he don't care about me or any of 'is other Fallen Divas, but he is who he is, innee? An' I've outgrown 'im in more ways than one. I can't put ma finger on it, but for some reason he just seemed to look a lot older. He gave me two hundred pounds an' sez I've gorra promise to come an' see 'im whenever I visit Nottingham. I sez, "Of course I will, ya silly old poof." But I know I'm never gonna see 'im again.

I'm gonna find ma place in the sun. They said that on *Rugrats* once. I din't know worrit meant. It must be nice feelin' like ya belong. We went to pick up Mammar Rita from the airport once an' when we saw the sign for 'ucknall on the way back she were like, "I love goin' away, but it's always nice to get 'ome again." An' I din't know what she were on about at first, coz we were still five minutes away from 'er house. But then I realized, she actually feels like 'ucknall is 'er home. An' I'm pleased she feels that way, coz I bet it's lovely to feel like that, but it's never bin *ma* home an' it never will be.

YOU GOT THE LOVE

Thanks for listenin', by the way. I guess I never really asked if ya wanted to 'ear all this. I just started rabbitin' on, eh? Mammar Joe used to say I could talk for England, me, an' I do waffle on, I know I do. It's like Smanfa always sez, a problem shared is a problem halved. She's a good egg, Smanfa. I'm lucky to have a mate like 'er. It does help, ya know, feelin' like there's someone listenin'. Coz it's bin lonely sometimes. But I can't be the only one who feels like this, canna? There must be people all over the country like me – all over the world! But ya just don't hear from us. I reckon we should talk about things more though, coz otherwise nothin'll change, an' it'll be like this for ever. An' I think there's summat better out there.

It's a pity I can't show Mammar Joe the railin's. Most o' the houses near the seafront have a floor at basement level, so there's fences to stop people fallin' down. I've gorra a basement flat. It's on a square. There's a park in the middle of it, like *EastEnders*. Ya can see the sea from the porch. There's railin's all over Brighton, actually. I saw 'em as we drove through, all old an' ornate, like the gates at Buckingham Palace. I bet no one down here is gonna appreciate 'em as much as me, coz I'm silly like that, aren't I? I love owt like that. I've always thought they should replace the railin's in 'ucknall, coz they could make it look dead good again, if they wanted to. Although I bet they weren't anywhere near as fancy as the ones down here.

The buildin's have got big, high windows too. Janet sez there's a lotta Regency architecture in Brighton an' that I should read up on the Prince Regent coz he's ma sorta person. It's gonna be amazin', I can just feel it – proper Sex an' the Seaside! Although I've bin thinkin' an' I've gorra stop speakin' like that, coz I reckon they'll all be dead posh at uni an' talk like Peter. I've bin practisin' the voice I'm gonna use if I wanna put ma hand up an' ask a question in lectures. I don't want 'em thinkin' I'm common. Or thick. I'm gonna reinvent mysen – I mean, *myself*. Like Madonna.

Michelle drove me down. Ma brother's mam. I'm quite touched, truth told. Sez it all though, don't it? First person in ma family to go to university an' someone else's mam's droppin' me off. Ma cousin's a heroin addict, for fuck's sake, but I'm the black sheep coz I like wearin' lipstick! Maybe I'd have gorra free pass if I sniffed glue an' fingered girls down Titchfield Park, but it's not ma style, is it? Honestly, they don't deserve me. I mean, I know I robbed someone an' that, but I've not done too bad to get mysen down here, have I?

Uncle John an' Aunty Louise are bringin' ma stuff tomorrow. I love Uncle John an' Aunty Louise. They're the only ones I really like from ma dad's side. He's got everythin' packed up in 'is van, but he's workin' late tonight, so they're comin' down in the afternoon. He works on the railways. I coulda just come wi' them, but

I've gorra be at registration dead early tomorrow. I'm gonna gerra taxi coz I can't be arsed workin' out public transport at that time o' the day. I'm quite far from campus, but I'm glad I've got ma own place. There's no way I can share wi' other people. I can't let anyone see me without makeup. An' I'm gonna have to make money. It's gonna be weird, innit, bein' in that induction tomorrow, lookin' round an' not knowin' who any of 'em are. Coz just think, in three years, everyone'll have an opinion on everyone else. People ya end up hatin'. People ya end up shaggin'. People ya end up bein' best mates with. Wonder what they'll make of me.

I've never bin this far south before. It feels dead far. Ya can't really get any further south. Michelle's gorra meetin' in London in the mornin', so she din't hang around to see ma apartment. I told 'er to get off coz it were dark by the time we got here, an' I'd already made us late settin' off, ya know worram like. She said the square looked nice an' to call 'er if there's any problems. I'll have to think of a way to thank 'er. I mainly talked about Mammar Joe on the way. I were makin' 'er laugh coz I told 'er I want it all – everythin' life has to offer – an' I'm gonna gerrit. But I do! An' I will. She reckons I'm crackers.

We had to collect the key when we arrived. The landlord seems a bit camp. There's gonna be a lot of 'em down here though, eh? I've read that people shout homophobic stuff at Brighton football matches, although I bet none o' the players are even gay coz there aren't any gay footballers, at least none that have come out. He din't say much, I reckon he just wanted to go to bed. Sez he's got some forms for me to fill in tomorrow. They sound dead posh down here.

The flat's dead bare. It sounds stupid, but the most excitin' part was openin' the fridge an' thinkin', This is *ma* fridge – this little fridge, here, in Brighton. An' I'll put *ma* milk in it to make *ma* cups of tea. I din't wanna put the big light on for some reason, so I just sat there wi' the fridge door open, an' thought about all the things I'm gonna do. It feels strange bein' in a completely different city. An' thinkin', This is ma home now. I hope I like it here, coz I'm not goin' back. I've slept with every man under thirty with an NG1 postcode. If I go back now, it's either celibacy or ma own sloppy seconds.

I've come out to sit by the sea now. It's a lot quieter than I thought it'd be, but it is Sunday. Well, Monday technically coz it's gone midnight. The nights are gerrin colder. I'm only a five-minute walk from the pier, the one that got burnt down, so I walk up. It's dead eerie. I'm not very good wi' distances, but I'd say it's about a hundred feet from the shore. I remember seein' it on *Blue Peter*. It's just sat there, rottin' away. Kinda reminds me of Byron in 'is crypt, all cold an' damp. It had a big ballroom at one point. They ought to rebuild it really, but I like how it's so dark, an' desolate. There's birds all over it. I wish I could fly up an' perch next to 'em. Imagine bein' there in the middle of a storm when one o' them beams falls down. I like the idea of summat so dramatic happenin' when no one's there to see it. There's so much we don't see.

Maybe I'll swim out there one day an' find a way up.

There's summat about the sea. Coz even if you've never seen it before – even if you've never heard of it – I feel like the sound o' the waves would still make sense, if ya know worra mean? Like it's waitin' for ya. An' as I'm sat here, listenin' to the waves crashin' in, I suddenly get this powerful sense that she's watchin' me. I feel a bit stupid at first, so I say it quietly.

Is that you, Old Mother 'ubbard?

I sez, I did it, Mammar. I made it out of 'ucknall.

I wish ya were here. I wish ya could see it.

It won't be the same without you, ya know.

I'm sorry I din't come an' see ya more. I hope ya know how much I love ya.

I'm gonna work hard, an' live ma life to the full. I'm gonna make ya proud.

I wish she could see how well I'm doin'. It's weird thinkin' about how much she's done for me, an' that she'll never see how well I've done gerrin all the way down here. I want 'er to know I'm a nice person, deep down, under this thick layer of bitch. I always thought I'd be able to repay 'er one day. She din't even know if I'd got ma A-levels. That's why I have to believe she's watchin' me. That she can see me bein' good.

I'd better get goin' back though, eh? I just wanna wake up an' feel good in the mornin'.

I'm gonna get some supplies tomorrow. Ma place is like Old bloody Mother 'ubbard's! Maybe I can borrow a cup o' sugar from ma neighbour. I saw 'im lookin' at me from the top flat when we pulled up. Talk about quick work, eh? He looked away when I caught 'im, but he were definitely checkin' me out. An' who can blame 'im? He's got eyes! Wonder if he knows ma little secret. Michelle sez I'm gonna end up causin' a commotion down here if I carry on the way I did in Notts, an' I daresay I could if I put ma mind to it. Mammar Joe used to say I could gerrin to trouble locked in a padded cell by mysen for five minutes, but she also used to say I'm not as green as I'm cabbage-lookin', so it's swings an' roundabouts, really. I hope she's not watchin' me *all* the time . . .

Acknowledgements

I'm afraid this is going to read a bit like an Oscar's acceptance speech. But writing a book is kind of a big deal for me and I simply couldn't have done it without the following people, in no particular order. I first went to Penguin with the idea for *What It Feels Like for a Girl* in 2013 (Olden Times) and I'm so grateful to Helen Conford for taking a chance on me. I was incredibly sad when she left Penguin. Thankfully Maria Bedford was there to pick up the reins so I've been blessed with not one wonderfully fantastic editor whom I'm proud to call a friend, but two. I'd also like to thank my long-suffering and lovely agent Rosemary Scoular, who frankly deserves an award for not throttling me by now, and dear David Dimbleby for introducing us. And indeed, to the whole gang at United Agents: especially Aoife Rice who never fails to provide a ray of light. Lockdown would have been unbearable without Natalia Lucas making time for my neurotic ramblings (and daily enquiries about invoices).

Special thanks to my publicist at Penguin, Isabel Blake, who has the patience of saint, Liz Parsons, who's bursting with ideas and kindness. I can't thank Caroline Dollimore and Sophie Brocklehurst at Cherry Create enough, thank you for helping me give birth to this. It's always so curious to me, when I log online, to read about the great 'conflict between trans women and REAL women' – when I've spent every day for the past decade supported by so many fantastic women.

There have been some men, too – Paul Flynn is of the male variety and also one of those people you're always enriched for having spoken with. Designer Tom Etherington is a Midlands lad who took on board my many ideas of what the cover should be: bold, gobby, unapologetic. Byron, in a word. We spent months obsessively creating *just* the right colour, something between a highlighter pen and an acid smiley, illuminated by public toilet fluorescent lighting. He's fantastic – give us an award.

I wasn't born into privilege and I only have a career thanks to people like Jane Czyzselska, certified good egg and the first person to pay me for my writing. Tim Lusher was the first person to put me in a newspaper, the *Guardian*'s *G2* magazine. Thanks for letting me do work experience at *Gay Times*, Tris Reid Smith. And Darren Scott for making me laugh. Thank you, Matthew Todd for pinching me for *Attitude*. It was a bit naughty – but so are you. Your book *Straight Jacket* had an enormous impact on me and many others. You don't come from privilege either and should feel really proud of everything you've achieved. I admire you.

Reni Eddo Lodge inspires me with the way she makes her voice heard, not only what she says but how she says it and the deep thought behind it. I've followed her career closely and learned so much from her – I'm also proud to call her a friend. Witty, kind-hearted Katherine O'Donnell was an early supporter of my work and is now a friend for life, whether she likes it or not. I'm also rather fond of her mother Joan.

Thank you, Alex Miller for offering me a column at *VICE* back when no one else thought trans people had anything interesting to say. I'm not sure my columns have all aged well, but we have. Cheers to everyone at *VICE*, actually: Amelia Abraham, Oz Katerj, Elektra Kotsoni, Eleanor Morgan, Sophie Heawood – I feel like I'm doing you all a disservice by listing you like this but I'm not sure what to say other than thank you for the warm welcome. Kev Kharas is a fantastic editor and would send copy back 20 per cent shorter and 50 per cent funnier without me being able to tell what he'd cut. Sam Taylor Smith's art sealed the deal. Another Midlands lad.

I really didn't want this to be one of those super long acknowledgements because honestly how tedious and self-absorbed, but I simply have to thank Edward Enninful, Giles Hattersley and Olivia Marks who literally changed my life when they opened the door at British *Vogue*. I'm so proud to write for such an exciting brand at such an exciting time under Edward's editorship. I've made many wonderful friends there, notably fellow Northerner and total gentleman Alec Maxwell and super talented MUA Niki M'nray. Then we have brave, bold Pippa Vosper (who has been so supportive of this book), fabulous, funny Susan Bender, thoughtful, fiercely intelligent Patricia Kingori and the impressive, flawless Vanessa Kingori – four absolute woman-crushes who I could talk to on the phone for hours, and often do.

Thank you so much to my family for supporting me to tell my story, in particular my mum and dad for giving me their blessing to speak my truth. It's not been easy for them to hear some of the things in this book, which is written from my perspective at a particular moment in my life. I'm pleased to say I have a great relationship with them in 2021. They want me to be happy and use my voice so children today like me don't go through what I went through – and parents like them might have more information on how to support us. I love you.

I'm forever grateful to my lovely Aunty, who is quite possibly the kindest and most principled person I have ever met. I love her to bits. Sarah Lennox has taught me so much about the world and is really a very sophisticated modern kind of gal. My Eminence Blonde. My Other Aunty is hilarious and has been a huge support to me along with my lovely uncle and cousin P. My beautiful sister isn't mentioned much in this book as we didn't grow up in the same house, but you have have always been there for me and I love you girl. I don't deserve you!

My brother-from-another-mother, I just couldn't be more proud of you and you've always embraced me for who I am. I know I must be missing off all sorts of people and will no doubt feel very stupid at some point. I have to thank pioneering trans women who inspired me early in my transition like Nadia Almada, Calpernia Addams, Christine Burns, and countless YouTubers who deepened my understanding of what I like to call our *predicament*. It's not easy being out there and I salute you and all the many others who have since come forward.

Thank you also to everyone who's spoken up for working people and for people like me (when they don't have to), too many friends to name here but Olly Alexander, Owen Jones and Ellie Mae O'Hagan spring to mind. Edouard Louis' writing has reignited my passion for reading and helped me to learn French over the past few years: he's so impressive. Merci beaucoup! Thank you also to Pandora Sykes for being so sisterly and one of the first people to shout about my book – it meant the world to me! May I say you have very good taste.

I'm not sure if it's appropriate to thank my grandmother as she's no longer here. Her words appear in this book as she wrote them. I never got to thank her properly but I think about her every day and the billions of women throughout history who've pushed their own needs aside while bending over backwards to care for others. The whole book is an acknowledgement to the power of that love and how it can transform a person. There are millions of Mammar Joe's out there who aren't valued as they should be for the important work they do in our society.

Thank you to Janet and Louai for all your love, talks and support over the years, lucky me to have met you. Thank you Alison at the Youth Offending Team and various social workers whose names I'm ashamed to have forgotten. Thank you to my English teacher with the furry coat, Justine Berry, the perfectly named Miss Kinder and Joanna Baker, my college tutor who fought hard for me to finish my A-levels. Mister Gallagher, I can't forget your jokes, nor can I repeat them. Thank you to everyone who works with young people and goes that extra mile for the Byrons of the world.

I can't go without thanking my best friend and ultimate bad influence, Steffi Moore, also known as 'Lady Die'. No one has ever had as much fun as we had in the early 2000s. Ever. They just haven't. I was absolutely terrified of making her the trope of the 'magical black person' – the mysterious Other who helps the white protagonist discover themselves. The truth is we discovered ourselves together, and I will forever be grateful for her brilliant mind, outrageous humour and heart of gold during a very difficult time in our lives. She is a trans woman of colour and deserves to have her voice heard on her own terms: the dialogue in this book is printed with her blessing and I hope she will join me on the publicity tour to speak in person too. I will be amazed if she can resist the attention. I can't wait for you all to meet her.

Finally, thank you to my fans, my followers, my friends from afar, some of whom have been following and supporting me for many years. I am touched and grateful for all the many messages I've received since Olden Times and am sorry to anyone I have not been able to respond to. I have one fan in particular, though, who believed me in me before anyone else, and he's been with me every step of the way. It's not a romance. It's more profound than that. This book wouldn't exist without him, and I might not either. If I live to be a hundred and the richest woman on earth, as I intend, I would never be able to repay him for what he's done for me. He's shy, so I won't name him here. Let's call him the mysterious Mister Duck. He knows who he is.